SMALL STEPS BIG OUTCOMES

How to change circumstances for success

MARNY CRINGLE

Copyright © 2022 Marny Cringle

Published by Disruptive Publishing
17 Spencer Avenue
Deception Bay QLD 4508
Australia

Cover design by Disruptive Publishing
Cover photo by Peter Stoop Photography
Back cover photo by Kerrie Anne Mathews
Editing by The Hawthorne Collective and Say It Write

All Rights Reserved. No part of this publication may be reproduced, distributed, stored in a retrieval system, or transmitted in any form or by any means, including photocopying, recording, or any other electronic methods, without prior written permission from the author, except as permitted under the Australian Copyright Act (for example, fair use for the purpose of study, research, criticism, or review). All enquiries should be made to the author, Marny Cringle.

This publication is a collection of the author's experiences and opinions only and is in no way intended to replace professional advice. Readers should seek advice from appropriate professionals before making any decisions based on the contents of this publication. To the maximum extent permitted by law, the author and publisher disclaim any responsibility or liability for the consequences of any actions resulting from the use of this book.

ISBN # 978-0-6455278-7-2 Print

A Note from the Author

At the end of each chapter, I have summarised things I have personally recognised and acknowledged, what I believe has helped me forge forward and get me through, or my beliefs that have developed from my life experiences. On occasions I have asked a question for you to consider.

This is not a training tool it is a story of my life experiences and how resilience, adaptability and determination has assisted me to get to where I am today.

CONTENT WARNING

This book contains graphic descriptions of **severe physical injury, domestic violence, and abuse.**

Some of these descriptions may be triggering. If you are impacted, please reach out to a friend, family member or support person, call a crisis hotline such as Lifeline Australia (13 11 14) or contact your local mental health support group or a professional in whom you trust.

Table of Contents

Chapter 1 – *Unexpected Trauma and Loss*   9

Chapter 2 – *Uncanny Coincidences*   13

Chapter 3 – *Childhood and Adolescence*   25

Chapter 4 – *Exciting Adventures*   55

Chapter 5 – *Uncertain Future*   75

Chapter 6 – *One Step at a Time*   111

Chapter 7 – *Sport and Music in Recovery*   129

Chapter 8 – *Patience and Determination*   143

Chapter 9 – *Strength in Adversity*   167

Chapter 10 – *Regaining Normality*   183

Chapter 11 – *Motivation and Persistence*   199

Chapter 12 – *Valuable Lessons*   213

Chapter 13 – *My Beneficial Traits*   233

Chapter 14 – *A Few Last Thoughts*   251

Conclusion   253

Acknowledgements   257

Chapter 1

Unexpected Trauma and Loss

The 1st of December 1996 was a typical Sunday evening in London.

I was waiting with a friend on an underground station platform, just like thousands of people do every evening.

However, this evening would turn out to be quite different, life changing ... to say the least.

A sturdy tube train came into the station and, as it did, it snatched me right off the platform and dragged me along.

It tore off my left leg and smashed my head in!

It knocked my eyes right out of their sockets!

It completely ripped out parts of my brain leaving me with massive head injuries and severe brain damage!

And, just for good measure, it broke my back in five places.

It then flung me down, smashed and shattered.

Unconscious, with virtually no chance of survival.

Just lying on the tracks, alone at death's door, waiting to die.

At the time of my accident, I was an ordinary person, probably very much like you, who just happened to be in the wrong place at the wrong time. Yet, through being forced to confront such terrible adversity, I discovered strength inside me that I had never guessed existed.

This story is my quest to recover from that terrible accident and recapture my life.

It is a true story. It is a story of incredible challenges and some amazing triumphs. It is a story about winning against all odds. It is a story about winning against the best opinions of the medical experts.

My story reveals my attitude towards my change in circumstances and what it did for me. It describes how I personally discovered that my life does not end just because my circumstances changed.

Chapter 1
Unexpected Trauma and Loss

Warning: I will be describing some horrific events that happened to me so that you can feel the gravity of my situation and how important and monumental it is that I overcame them. There will be graphic descriptions of abuse, physical injury and domestic violence.

My story highlights that when challenges occur, I alter my approach to reaching my goal, not my decision to attain it. I believe success is not a place where you want to be, it is a journey, and I am about to tell you about my incredible journey and how my outlook and mindset impacted on outcomes.

Chapter 2

Uncanny Coincidences

The train accident in London was not the first time that my life's direction had been dramatically changed due to an unfortunate accident. Twenty-five years earlier, when I was just twenty months old, my thirty-one-year-old father had also been in the wrong place at the wrong time resulting in him being involved in a serious accident. My father's accident not only totally changed his life but also the lives of my mother, my brothers and, of course, my life too.

Older relatives and friends of my parents have often told me about my dynamic mother and father back when they were in their teens. Even today, they still talk about them, usually starting with something like: "Oh! Your mother and father…" and then going on to describe the dances that were held at the Maitland Town Hall in their youth and how Mum and Dad would tear up a storm on the dance floor.

By all accounts Dad was the most eligible young bachelor in town. He was handsome and charming, and an absolute gentleman with a great potential future. All the girls were chasing him but he only had eyes for my mother.

Their relationship progressed over time and on the eighth of January 1966, they were married. Their genuine love for one another was intense and their presence together was noticeable and electrifying. Dad moved around with his work and so, after they were married, Mum joined him in South Australia and then later they moved to Wollongong, NSW, for a position that Dad had accepted there. Everything was going along like a dream.

Bertram and Robyn Cringle on their wedding day 8.1.66

They decided to start a family and had two sons and me, their only daughter and second born child.

Dad had established himself as a much in demand Constructional Engineer who managed and supervised construction within the mining industry and was receiving a colossal salary. He also had an excellent retirement program and he often told Mum that they would be living in clover, not only throughout their working life but also into old age.

At that time Dad was working in Bulli coal mine. Mum and Dad were also building their dream home and Mum was pregnant with child number four. They were still very much in love and life could not be better.

With everything going so well they could never have guessed that their lives were soon going to change drastically as a result of Dad being the victim of a terrible accident that was considered to be one of Australia's most horrific car accidents at that time.

Chapter 2
Uncanny Coincidences

On the day of the accident Dad and his boss were driving back from a work conference in Sydney. Unbeknown to them two teenage boys in a stolen car were racing along and would soon lose control of their vehicle. The car thieves rolled the car they were driving, and Dad's car just happened, by total chance, to be in the exact wrong position in Cataract Creek at that point in time. The rolling stolen car landed right on top of them on 18 August 1971. The thieves were not charged for their foolish actions and later moved on to commit one of the most gruesome murders known in Australian history.

His boss was killed in the horrific accident and Dad received such severe brain damage that he was hospitalised for two and a half years. Initially, the doctors did not expect Dad to survive. He was unconscious for eight months and for the first three and a half months, he was on life support. Even though he survived and was eventually released from hospital, he required twenty-four-hour care for the rest of his life.

As I said above, Mum was pregnant at the time of Dad's accident, but seven months into the pregnancy she miscarried. This was probably due to the stress and emotional pressures resulting from the accident. So, at one point in time Mum was in the same hospital as Dad, however he was still unconscious during that time. The unborn baby that they lost had been another boy, but he never got the chance to have a life.

Just imagine for a moment the full effect of Dad's accident. Not only on my successful father himself, but also on my mother. Without warning the man Mum loved was smashed beyond recognition and laying in hospital, unconscious and in a critical condition. For months Mum did not even know whether Dad was going to live or die. Mum's dream life, that she had been living since marrying Dad, was whipped out from under her and replaced with a life of hardship and sacrifice. She lost her unborn child, she had to shoulder all the responsibility for raising my two brothers and myself, and with little money to do it with. As well, she became my father's constant carer for the next thirty-six years, until he passed away on 7 December 2007. This was not the married life that Mum had signed up for, but the way she coped with it was inspiring.

Mum never once complained about the difficulties of caring for my father and three children, but as she got older the ramifications of being a constant 24-hour carer for my father was taking its toll on her physically. Mum rarely had respite and during a couple of days of one respite occasion in 2007, the service did not care for Dad appropriately which then resulted in him being hospitalised and subsequently dying at home. Dad loved Mum intently and appreciated everything she did for him. Dad's last words directly spoken to me before he declined into unconsciousness were: "I love you… look after your mother."

Dad impacted my life immensely and he regularly vocalised how grateful he was to be alive and continue to be a part of the life of his family. I have nothing but total respect and admiration for the way my mother adapted to those terrible, unplanned life changes. She devoted herself to Dad, who had multiple disabilities, and to raising my brothers and me in such a way as to ensure that we never missed out on anything and that we were never disadvantaged by the circumstances.

People often say that *sometimes* bad things in life have a good side as well, and I think that is true. Looking back on my parents and my childhood I can see now, how watching the way both my parents coped with the challenges that they had been thrown,

Chapter 2
Uncanny Coincidences

helped develop my own character. I am sure that the way in which I could tap into hidden strengths after my own accident was due in a large part to having those particular parents and the particular childhood experiences they gave me.

The brain damage that Dad received left his intellect intact, but it severely affected his physical functioning. He had great difficulty walking but could manage it with the aid of a walking stick, although going up or down steps posed a challenge for him. Later in life this ability deteriorated, and he was confined to a wheelchair.

The brain damage also resulted in Dad having difficulty speaking. He would try to express himself in the least number of words and, even then, most people could not understand what he was saying. But having grown up with him, we could understand him.

I was always amazed by Dad's ability to express detailed thoughts or observations in just a few words. It is testament to his full intelligence still being there, despite the damage the accident had done to other functions.

It must have been so frustrating for Dad after his accident. Before the accident he was a successful young man with a good career, well liked socially, he enjoyed dancing, and apparently had been an exceptionally good sportsman. I have been told that at one time he made the shortlist for selection into the Australian Diving Squad to go to the Commonwealth Games. Being a good dancer and a diver, he must have had a high degree of co-ordination, yet, because of the car accident, he was forced to live in a body that had huge difficulty with co-ordination.

I was too young to remember much of when Dad first came out of hospital, but what I do clearly remember of my father is a man who was always laughing. He had an incredibly positive attitude and was grateful for all that he still had, and he did not dwell on what he had lost. He loved his children and took great pleasure in seeing us having fun.

This is me in infancy… while Dad was in hospital

Dad was a Catholic and Mum converted to Catholicism when she married Dad. Therefore, we were raised as Catholics and the five of us would attend church every Sunday. Due to Dad's mobility issues, we always sat in the front seat so the Eucharist could be brought to him. Every Sunday whilst in church Dad was very emotional throughout the service and would often cry wholeheartedly. I was never embarrassed by Dad's emotional outbursts; I was just pleased to see that he could be affected so deeply in such a positive light.

Despite the chaos around me growing up and the fact that Dad was disabled, I saw him as normal. I accepted the fact that Dad had his injuries and restrictions. That is just how it was. Our

Chapter 2
Uncanny Coincidences

family was a normal family, and our parents were great parents. I am still happy and grateful today for what my parents did for us.

Dad was always giving compliments to both Mum and me. I remember him often saying things like: "Ooh la la," and: "You're beautiful." He loved my mother, Robyn, intently and really appreciated all the things she did. He would often tell her with intense emotion: "You're wonderful, Rob!"

Straight after his accident Dad was placed in hospital in Sydney and he was not expected to survive the horrific accident given his extensive brain injury and other injuries. We then moved to Sydney, to be near the hospital, so we could visit him regularly. When he eventually came out of hospital, we all moved to Maitland, NSW, to be close to my mother's mother – my Nan.

Nan and Mum were remarkably close, and I have many fond memories from my childhood of time spent with Nan. There was always lots of laughing, music, dancing and fun.

I have sentimental memories of my energetic Nan who brought up four young children on her own as her husband, my mother's father, was killed in a car accident when Mum was only 10 years old. Another blow that Nan had to deal with was living through several floods where water levels were above the ceiling of the family home. Thankfully, she remained in this house where Mum grew up and Christmas would always be at Nan's where we would dance and be merry. Fun and laughter surrounded my cheerful Nan who was a tremendous support for my small-framed mother when we returned to Maitland after my father's accident. Nan was noticeably young at heart and taught me to not become too worried about material things, but in preference place infinite value on being genuine and to reveal the goodness in your heart.

Mum made sure that that my brothers and I never missed out on anything in childhood. We played a variety of sports. We learned music. I learned dancing and performed in various public concerts both as a dancer and as a musician. I think we probably did more than any other children I knew.

When other people get to know my story and Dad's story, they are usually amazed at the number of uncanny coincidences that occurred twenty-five years apart.

We both loved and excelled at sport before our accidents, and we lived highly active lives. Both accidents were due to chance events that caused us to be in the wrong place at the wrong time. We each received extensive brain damage and were each unconscious for an extended period after the accident. We were both on life support, and in each case the doctors did not expect us to survive, but we both survived against the odds.

We have each taken the point of view that surviving against the odds is symbolic of having a second life. In each case our life after the accident was quite different to the life we were living before the accident. We each had new challenges to face and new problems to solve that would determine the course that our new lives followed.

I think that it is also interesting that my father had his near-death accident in Australia, the country where I was born, whereas I had my near-death accident in England, the country of my father's birth.

Chapter 2
Uncanny Coincidences

One major difference between us is that I fully recovered from the brain damage whereas unfortunately Dad did not. However I think that my determination to recover and resume a normal life was in a large part inspired by having grown up seeing what it is like to not fully recover from such damage. As a result I was determined that my life was not going to be one of dependence on others, like my father's unfortunately was, sadly due to the actions of delinquents.

At the time of Dad's accident it seemed that no-one really believed that the brain could repair itself after major damage. Dad was an incredibly positive person who had a great attitude to life even after his accident. He focused on what he did have and what he could do rather than feeling sorry for himself.

Even today no-one yet knows for certain why one patient fully recovers from serious brain damage whereas another one does not. Apparently, one of the brain experts in London, when commenting on the speed at which I was recovering, said that the brains of musicians are much better at repairing brain damage than are those of non-musicians. I have been playing violin seriously from a young age and that may well have helped. But I think that being a musician is just part of the explanation.

Science is only just beginning to understand the power of self-belief and a positive attitude throughout patient recovery. I think that self-belief and a positive attitude played a strong role in helping me to recover, return to my nursing career and achieve my goal of living a normal life again.

I think that some people are lucky enough to have had examples and experiences throughout childhood that allowed them to naturally develop inner strength, whereas others develop their inner strength later in life from their own efforts. Whichever way

Small Steps
Big Outcomes

it happens for you it is well worth developing that strong inner character.

As a result of my experiences since my accident I have come to believe that, in so many ways, your character is your destiny!

Me playing my violin in London, shortly before my accident

Chapter 2
Uncanny Coincidences

- Sometimes bad things in life have a good side.

- Personal character and tapping into hidden strengths that developed from childhood experiences.

- Positive attitude and gratefulness.

- Normality is different for everyone … that is just how it is.

- The power of self-belief and a positive attitude.

- Developing inner strength.

Chapter 3

Childhood and Adolescence

You may be disturbed by some of the information I am about to reveal. This part of my life is very unsettling, but little did I know that this harrowing time would lead to the development of multiple powerful traits that would benefit me, not only when dealing with challenges, but in many other aspects of my life.

When I was four and a half years old Dad finally came home from hospital and the whole family moved to Telarah, a suburb of Maitland in the Hunter Valley, NSW. We lived in that rental house for the next seven years, basically all my infant and primary school days.

It was during this time that I learnt to survive, to fend for myself and be totally alone with how I dealt with things and without mentioning a word! I was surrounded by people who cared for me, but I was frightened and for my own safety, I could not display this.

Unfortunately, I was sexually abused by a relative for seven long and daunting years. Even before I started school, I had to make Marny a survivor. From this young age I learnt how to get on with things, without being any different from anyone else, and simply carry on as though everything was normal. I can certainly relate to the graceful swan analogy where outwardly things appear to be moving gracefully but under the surface my thought processes were in chaotic turmoil. Luckily for me, what was beneath the surface was powerful. I just kept telling myself that I can and will get through this!

Some little girls automatically gravitate toward playing with dolls and other traditionally girly type of games, but that certainly was not me. If I had to choose one word to describe myself as a young child, I would have to pick active. When you have two brothers and no sisters you learn pretty soon that you have to be able to play as rough and tough as they do, or you are going to get swamped – and there was no way that I was ever going to get swamped by anyone.

When we were at home my brothers and I were generally in the back yard kicking a ball or playing cricket. Or we would be on our

Chapter 3
Childhood and Adolescence

bikes riding up and down the street. I had little interest in indoor pastimes such as watching television. I felt safer if I were outside in the open and actively running around where people could see me, particularly in winter, when my abuser would present to our house a couple of times throughout the week after football practice. Even when the video game craze came along in the 1970's my brothers would often be in their rooms playing whatever game was popular at the time, but I would still be doing something more active outside.

Mum was determined that my brothers and I would not be disadvantaged because of Dad's accident and so we lived a highly active lifestyle. We played a variety of competition sports, and I also did ballet, tap dancing and even Polish Dancing. Looking back on it now, it seems like we were almost always involved in some activity, or we were driving to or from some activity. It appeared to me that many other children I knew did not have as active, involved lives that we did.

My brothers played with the local soccer and cricket clubs, and we all did swimming and athletics. I was not interested in team sports and felt I could vent some of my frustrations if I played a sport where I could transfer some of my resentment and confusion. I then started playing tennis at a young age and I would often be swimming laps in the Maitland pool and competing in racing events with the swimming club on Friday nights.

When I went to athletics, I would participate in every event they had. It did not matter to me whether it was sprinting, jumping, throwing or running, I enjoyed it all. However my favourite events were the High Jump and the distance races. I even made a high jump set for home and would often be having fun practicing in the yard.

During my primary school years we were always doing something. Mum would be driving us to one thing or another and Dad, the boys and I would all be in the car. After Dad's accident Mum wanted to have the safest car to drive us all around in and eventually decided on buying a pale blue Volvo. It was a 244GL model and I remember the number plate, JIV 800, and I would appropriately be *jiving* around in the car. Our home environment was often chaotic and terribly busy, especially with Dad rehabilitating over several years. Regardless of the pandemonium, Mum ensured that she got us to all the various activities we were involved in, and I still had enough time to do homework, practice the violin and regularly play chess and draughts with Dad.

We were particularly busy on weekends. If we were not at some sporting event or other commitment, then we would be visiting Nan at her place or we would drive to Shoal Bay for the day. We often drove to Katoomba, about two hundred kilometres away, to visit Mum's grandparents. I clearly remember those long drives with Eagles music playing on the car tape deck.

I have lots of great memories of time spent at Nan's place. We often climbed the large tree in her back yard, especially when the Maitland Show was on, and we would have a bird's eye view of most of the showground and the Ferris wheel.

Chapter 3
Childhood and Adolescence

Me and Nan (Marjorie) dancing on Christmas Day 1989

I had to do all the cans throughout the abuse: I can do this: I can do that and so on. I did not want to be overpowered or taken advantage of. I was just terrified of what more would happen if I did not do as he requested. My psyche developed into one of survival and to deal with things the best way I could – alone and without telling anyone. I simply had to be like that to survive. My view was that if I survived today tomorrow would come. One step at a time.

I was extremely perplexed when I saw him – my abuser - with his girlfriend, where he would be openly affectionate and loving towards her. But with me, he was not so loving or as nice when others were not around. I was forced to join him in scheming ways to be alone together unnoticed. When we were alone, which was frequently, he was at times threatening whilst also gently explaining why things were different between us.

It was in my final year of primary school, during a sex education talk, that I horrifically discovered what this disgusting man was doing to me when he came to our home a couple of times a week after football or at family gatherings. After I realised that he was abusing me I felt as though my insides had been ripped out of me. I was ashamed of myself for not having the courage to stop his forceful demands. My anger and frustrations then gave me power and determination to put an immediate stop to him abusing me.

I clearly remember the last night when this conniving relative came into my room, and I yelled out to Mum who unfortunately did not hear me. He frantically left my bedroom and knew himself that it was over – he appeared to be petrified of what I was potentially capable of. Due to more threats however, I was then afraid to say anything to anyone and just had to go on living my life. He soon moved, with his family, to a different area but I continued to suffer in silence and did not reveal what this disgraceful man did to me for fear of what would happen. I managed to get by, despite the pain that I carried and the hurt within my subconscious.

I liked the thought of creating music and the joy it could bring, but feel I also gravitated towards wanting to play the violin as I was attracted to the beautiful sound of the violin as it soothed me. I question myself at times, did I start playing the violin as a form of soothing therapy to deal with my abuse and take my mind off the negative effects?

Chapter 3
Childhood and Adolescence

I had made a firm decision at five years old to play the violin and enthusiastically approached Mother Pauline for lessons. However, with encouragement, this elderly nun with a black and white veil, suggested that I would progress more if she started teaching me when I was older and had better concentration skills, especially when reading. I was disappointed but rather than get sad about not playing the violin, I thought this sounded like a wise approach to getting me to where I wanted to be. This dear old nun had suggested a thoughtful solution to creating the effect I was aiming for.

Playing the violin was always in the back of my mind when I committed myself to gradually improving my concentration, persisting with the necessary steps required to prepare myself and enjoying myself throughout the process to encourage my enthusiasm and motivate my intentions.

After three years of continuous efforts, receiving positive comments from school teachers in relation to my progress and personally noticing my improvement, I felt I was well prepared to start playing the violin and that Mother Pauline would confirm how much I had progressed.

It was during term two of third class when I proudly approached this worldly nun with excitement. As it was well into the year and systems were in place, she informed me that it would be best if I started violin lessons when school commenced the next year. From nine years of age, I finally connected with the violin that allowed me to express my emotions and provided light-hearted joy as I gradually improved.

Mum often commented that she would never have to ask me to practice my violin, it was just something I did willingly every day.

It was a relief to be connected to something that brought me so much comfort.

At the end of primary school, we moved to a new house that was designed by a reputable Sydney architect and built to suit Dad's needs. I lived there throughout my high school years and Mum and Dad lived there for the rest of their lives. For me, our new home represented many new beginnings in relation to freedom and inner strength.

Our new house in the Hunter Valley was purpose-designed to be level because we knew that Dad would end up in a wheelchair as he got older. The house was in a very pleasant location with plenty of grass both front and back and good 360-degree views. Our beautiful and modern family home was certainly in a wonderful location.

Chapter 3
Childhood and Adolescence

Because we had so much open grass we needed a ride-on mower. My brothers were not interested in mowing the grass, but I was more than happy to race around on the ride-on mower doing the lawn. It was a lot more fun than being inside helping with the housework!

Here I am mowing, in January 1988

Bolwarra Heights was a great place to live, but it had its share of snakes, who also thought it was a good place to live. These were mostly red-bellied black snakes, and, what the locals simply call the brown snake, that is more correctly named the eastern brown snake. The red-bellied black snake is quite venomous, but most people who are bitten by one do not die from the poison. The eastern brown snake, despite its simple name, is the world's second most venomous land snake and is responsible for around 60% of all Australian snake bite deaths. Both these breeds of snake are often found on farms and around rural houses in Eastern Australia, including Bolwarra Heights. From time to time one of these snakes may even slither into a house hoping to find a juicy mouse hiding there, so, if you live in a snake area you may have an unwanted encounter.

Mum did not like snakes, but she was remarkably cool under pressure. One day she was hanging clothes on the line and when she went back into the laundry she was confronted with the sight of a large, red-bellied black snake curled across the tiles of the laundry floor. Snakes can be dangerous if they are trying to escape and their path to freedom is blocked. Luckily, Mum was a quick thinker. She calmly reached out and placed her hands on the edge of the laundry tub and then by leaning her weight over the tub she lifted her legs off the floor and allowed the snake a means of escape. The snake seized the opportunity and quickly left the laundry for greener pastures. I feel it was Mum's fortitude, strength of mind and quick-thinking that saved her from being bitten.

When I was sixteen years old, I had my own snake encounter. It happened one day while riding my horse, Felicity, around the neighbouring paddocks. It was not uncommon for snakes to be in the grass in those paddocks, but that was not usually a problem because whenever the wild birds would see a snake, they would go crazy with warning cries, and all their friends would join in the chorus. On this day however the birds let us down.

Chapter 3
Childhood and Adolescence

Felicity was a beautiful horse with a lovely nature, and she would prance around excitedly whenever she knew we were about to leave our property to go riding together. This day we were galloping around nearby paddocks and at one point we gracefully jumped over a fallen tree trunk. However, while we were sailing through the air, we both looked down simultaneously and to our mutual horror saw that there was a mother brown snake, complete with her babies, lying on the top of that very log. Felicity was so close to the snake, as we sailed across the log, that she might have even brushed it with a hoof.

Felicity became startled as soon as she saw that snake and somehow, she shied mid-air with the result that we landed awkwardly, and I fell off. Felicity then bravely high-tailed it out of there and immediately headed for home, leaving me to socialise with mother snake. Brown snake mothers are notoriously aggressive when they have young snakes to protect and so I was in genuine danger of being bitten and injected with deadly snake venom.

I do not know exactly what speed my heart rate hit at that moment, but I could tell it was galloping at a speed greater than Felicity when she high tailed it home. I had visions of the snake launching itself at me from the grass and striking with deadly force and purpose. To make matters worse I now could not see where the snake was, but I was not hanging around to investigate. I was a good runner, and on that day I made such a lightning bolt escape that I wouldn't have been surprised if I'd managed to pass Felicity on the way home!

When I did arrive home, I found Felicity in the back paddock and spent some time soothing her down and then, deciding that I had reached my excitement limit for the day, I went inside the house to lay on our comfortable lounge and recover. Our house had high ceilings with a long skylight. The lounge was right under the skylight, and it was a very pleasant place to lie back and relax for a well-earned rest and a chance to recover from my harrowing ordeal.

Jarnah and Felicity in the back yard

I had been lying there for a short while and I was starting to relax again when I heard a thud and felt something had landed between my legs. Mum had a good sense of humour and I thought she was playing a prank on me. I looked behind to where Mum was sitting, but she was reading something with a serious look on her face and was clearly not joking with me. I then looked down at my legs and there was a young brown snake that had somehow gotten up onto one of the rafters in the skylight and fallen directly onto me! It is frightening enough to be lying in the grass close to a deadly mother brown snake but, believe me, you reach a whole new level of fear when you are up close and personal with the world's second most venomous snake lying between your legs on the lounge!

I am sure you have heard the expression scared stiff, well that second brown snake encounter, within about 20 minutes of the first one, froze me as solid as a statue. That turned out to be a

Chapter 3
Childhood and Adolescence

good reaction to have because the snake then slid away under my left thigh and into the lounge.

Then, for the second time that day I was into lightning-fast snake-avoidance mode. I can assure you that I was not even tempted to use the calm, relaxed, style that Mum had shown when escaping the snake in the laundry. No way! I frantically jumped up and ran to the cupboard and grabbed a broom to protect myself in case the mother brown snake was nearby.

I called the police and they arrived at the house several hours later and carried the comfortable green lounge, complete with the snake passenger inside it, out onto the veranda with two acres of surrounding bush. They explained their theory that the snake would naturally leave the lounge at some point and happily go back into the outside world where it belonged.

I do not how long that lounge remained on the veranda, but I can tell you that I did not sit on that lounge again for years.

The first few years after moving to Bolwarra Heights were the years where I started to set some direction in my life. I started high school at St Joseph's College, Lochinvar, which was also a convent and boarding school. I was a day pupil and travelled for over an hour to and from school each day. I met some girls when I was in Year 7 throughout 1982 who became great lifelong friends who remain connected to my life today. I also discovered that I had some natural ability for cross country and long distance running and I really enjoyed it. I also started playing violin in an orchestra, something that I still do to this day. And, because I needed to choose which subjects to study, I made a firm decision that nursing would be my career. I always had a passion to become a nurse which required me to study biology and chemistry, I only studied these because I was committed to the cause. Nursing was my true calling.

High school was an all-girls school. It was situated on beautiful grounds surrounded by rolling hills and had a mixture of day students and boarders. It was attached to a convent housing the Sisters of St Joseph, who are remarkably kind, open, compassionate and with many more endearing qualities. The school also had an excellent music department named after St Cecilia (the patroness of music). It was in a rural environment and had a swimming pool, tennis court and there was plenty of land around the school. I would generally arrive at school early and either swim laps in the pool or go for a cross country run around the Stations of the Cross or up to the *Mushroom Tree* and back.

The Stations of the Cross depicted the events of Jesus' journey to crucifixion and were fourteen large white crosses dug into the ground on various locations on the hillside. The *Mushroom Tree* was our name for a large tree that resembled a giant mushroom and was alone on the top of a steep hill that was a good distance away for a morning run.

By far my favourite memories of high school revolve around social time spent down the back of the school, past the dairy, during lunch or the morning break, talking, joking and laughing with my friends. They were a positive group of girls, well-educated and harmonious and we got on very well. With all the challenges I was forced to confront, both during school and after my accident, it was a comfort to know that I had good, strong friendships to rely on whenever I needed them. My wonderful

Chapter 3
Childhood and Adolescence

friends are like-minded people who encourage me and have genuinely been there throughout both the good and bad times.

My school friends and I had a lot in common and we enjoyed our times together, but one big difference between us was that they never discovered the joy of running that came so naturally to me. I can remember that during physical education (PE) we often had to run up to the *Mushroom Tree*. My dear friends were not too enthusiastic about expending their energy this way, so while I ran up to the tree through long grass, small valleys and passing a cow here and there, my friends would have much delight resting, waiting, and laughing in a gully amongst the trees in one of the paddocks. After I had completed the run, I would make my return to school via the gully that they were waiting in. They would take that as the signal to wait a short while and start walking back to the school grounds, making sure that they went at a faster pace when nearing the school, arriving breathless, red faced and exhausted, looking as though they had just completed a challenging run.

Unfortunately the PE teacher cottoned on to what we were doing. So, to enable her to be aware of who supposedly ran up to the *Mushroom Tree*, a stamp was placed at the base of the tree, and we had to stamp our wrists to show we had made the trek.

So that my dear friends did not have to put their fragile bodies through too much torture, we then devised a new plan of action.

After I had stamped my wrist, I ran back down throughout the paddocks and reached the gully where my friends were waiting, we would wet my wrist and I would carefully place my wrist over theirs to achieve an authentic stamp that indicated that they also completed the run. Our little scheme worked so well that one of my friends was actually chosen to represent the school at a cross country event, an opportunity which she tactfully declined.

Today I can do almost everything that I could do before my accident but the one thing I cannot do anymore is run. I am grateful that I took the opportunity to really enjoy running during my teenage years.

I will always cherish my time at high school simply because of the genuine friendships I made. I also feel that those relationships I built during my high school years will remain a valuable part of my life. I can honestly say that true friendships never end, and that the close friendships I formed at high school will be part of my life forever. Every one of us has travelled down different paths and led hectic lifestyles, however we all still manage to meet up throughout the year to share our stories and naturally enquire how each of us is travelling throughout life. There is such a unique and special bond between us all!

The positive guidance I received at school allowed me to be elected as class captain and sports captain. I still have my school badge of St Joseph's College, Lochinvar. On it is written our motto of *Vigor in Arduis* which can be translated as strength in the face of difficulties, hardships or adversity. It is fascinating how these three words have positively influenced my approach to dealing with the various challenges I have dealt with over the past forty years. An affirmation that continues to serve me.

During my high school years, I was fortunate to form a strong bond with many Sisters of St Joseph, particularly Sister Agnes, Sister Anita and Sister Lauretta. Sister Agnes was a dear friend

Chapter 3
Childhood and Adolescence

and remarkable teacher – like my own mother her determination and wisdom guided me to acknowledge the positive aspects of my life, develop my abilities to their full potential and simply do the best that I could.

Whenever I trained for cross country during my lunch breaks Sister Agnes would ensure I had safely returned to the school after running up to the *Mushroom Tree* or along Station Lane and that I was well hydrated before returning to class. Sister Anita and Sister Lauretta also made a long-standing imprint in my heart and motivated me to be courageous in my pursuits. I am truly fortunate and appreciative of the relationships I formed and the valuable lessons and experiences gained whilst a student at St Joseph's College Lochinvar. Collectively they helped to shape my outlook and approach to life. The Sisters of St Joseph remain part of my life and I am grateful for their prayers, blessings and support. As outlined by Father Tension Woods in 1868: *'Sisters of St Joseph should have great courage, a courage that rises with difficulties and obstacles instead of being lessened by them.'* The Josephite's certainly embody this courage and continue to never see a need, however big or small, without doing something about it. They do what they can to help others and represent justice, perseverance, genuine openness, hospitality, generosity, kindness and support.

I was never overly interested in the academic side of school, but I always did well because I had the habit of doing whatever homework and study I was required to do. This habit has served me well throughout my life. There have been many times, particularly since my accident, when I needed to do things that I would have preferred to avoid. In those situations, I simply put my head down and did what I must. I think that developing the habit of doing what needs to be done, when it needs to be done is an important ingredient in achieving personal success in any endeavour.

During my primary school years, I was always busy with some activity or another and this pattern continued into my high school years as well. I participated in various sporting activities and enjoyed lots of success with it. I did competition swimming, played A-grade tennis, did athletics, and competed very successfully in cross country running and local fun runs. I represented the school many times in running and on the weekends, I often competed in fun runs against adults and usually won. I really enjoyed winning, but I also enjoyed the sheer freedom of running. When I was running, I would soon be out in the lead, and I had the feeling that I was in total control of my situation and doing exactly what I wanted to do without anyone else telling me to do it this way or that way. I was free to be myself and I loved the feeling.

Throughout high school I was persistent and took continuous actions to get where I wanted to be and not let the awful experiences relating to my abuse hinder my development. It was my final year at primary school that I discovered the extent of my abuse, and it was my final year at high school that my mother became aware of what I endured in my younger years.

When I was in Year 11 at high school a counsellor came to the school talking about abuse. It made sense to make enquiries with this trusted individual. I did not give this lady my name or address but months later, at the beginning of Year 12, I received a letter from her.

I was incredibly angry towards this professional woman for sending me a letter, and was I confused, bewildered, annoyed and troubled by her actions. Unfortunately, Mum opened this

Chapter 3
Childhood and Adolescence

letter, and one evening after everyone had gone to bed, she came into my room to ask me what the letter was about. After I had said something to the effect that it was for an assignment at school, there was a bit of a heated argument, and Mum eventually rang the convent to speak with Sister Loretta, who was the school principal. In the middle of the night, to get to the bottom of this, Mum insisted we drive out to the convent and discuss matters with Sister Loretta. This was the first time my Mum had discovered what had occurred to me and by whom. What a devastating blow for a devoted mother, who was very protective of her children that she loved. I had immense inner turmoil but did not verbalise my feelings or the devastating things that happened to me as a child to anyone, including my dear friends. This was a secret that only four people knew about: Mum, Sister Loretta, me, and the abuser.

My final year at school was difficult and emotional, but I had good people around me. I had supportive friends to hold my spirits up. Whilst at school I did not tell any of them about my abuse and what I was currently faced with. Internally it was crushing me, but I just took it in my stride. During my final year of high school when I was studying for my Higher School Certificate, and felt my future depended on my input, I was battling with why the abuse happened and asking myself: "What did I do?"

Only recently my dear friend Marian, who I am remarkably close to and have had the pleasure of knowing for forty years, informed me of something that happened in Year 12 at a religious school camp. Marian told me that when we were bunking in a room together, I woke up screaming and said: "Stop it!" and I was and crying. Marian thought I left the room to see a teacher. What had actually happened was that I ran away from the camp.

When I was battling with my conflicted emotions, I told two individuals who I knew and thought I could trust: Father Hart and Father Wilson. It was during a very brief conversation with Father Hart at the religious Camp that I told him that I was abused. In response he said: "What did you do to lead him on?" I was so distraught by his comment that I ran away from the camp in order to deal with my emotions and get away from a man who blamed me for what had tragically occurred to me for so long during my childhood.

Shortly after this camp, enraged, I went to see another priest who frequently visited our home, Father Wilson. When I told him what Father Hart said, initially he made no comment, then absurdly agreed with what Father Hart had said to me previously, saying "So what did you do to start it?"

This was the third time I had reached out to someone to tell them about my nightmare, and this is how I was treated. After this I came to believe that some things are best left unsaid. I had reached out to a counsellor and then two priests to help make some sense of what occurred to me, and on all three occasions I was made to feel like I had done something wrong. I then decided that it was important for me to be assertive. I knew that despite the pain I carried and how much hurt and turmoil remained in my subconscious, I would get though.

The year after this all happened, when I was studying my first year at university, I decided that I was going to press charges against this abhorrent man who had abused me from the age of four to nearly twelve. To my dismay this did not occur as he was

Chapter 3
Childhood and Adolescence

killed in an accident. This was both a time that was bitter and sweet for me.

An uncanny coincidence was that my abuser was killed in an accident on the first of the month by a train where he lost both of his legs. I was also involved in an accident where I was hit by a train on the first of the month and lost one of my legs plus a host of other horrific injuries. I feel that this insolent man has paid the price for his actions whereas my survival represents how consolidating my inner strength and approach to achieving what I want out of life will inspire and influence others to be determined to succeed and just move forward and do what it takes.

I learned more about resilience after that hardship. As a child I learnt to suffer quietly and just keep moving forward. I have certainly gained wisdom from my hardships.

A marvellous woman who was well educated and very uplifting was a dear teacher at school, Sister Agnes. She once commented that: "Everyone has a gift: we have a purpose in life, and we are going to do good ... use your strengths and help the world." I know I have become powerfully strong from what has occurred in my past and have been determined, for as long as I can remember, to get to where I want to be.

From an early age I have internalised and dealt with things the best way I can. With challenges, be they personal or in my working life, I have faced them with the same approach of being meticulous, patient and grateful of small wins or positive occurrences.

Small Steps
Big Outcomes

It was during high school that I had one of the most memorable, enjoyable and rewarding experiences of my life. I joined the local youth group.

An amazing woman, Joy, ran a local youth group every Monday night. Joy was a professional ice-skater who had previously worked and travelled with vaudeville artists that consisted of ten to fifteen individual unrelated acts that featured acrobats, magicians, jugglers, comedians, trained animals, singers and dancers. Thankfully, Joy formed a local group for teenagers, both boys and girls, and I joined this group when I was about twelve years old and remained in it until my senior years of high school.

Joy is a woman of boundless energy, creativity and enthusiasm. We would put on shows throughout the local communities (and when I say shows I mean mini spectaculars). There would be jugglers, unicycle riders, musicians, dancers and whoever Joy could entice onto our stage. She had a great skill of getting the most out of each one of us and making it lots of fun in the process. She always seemed to be able to find a way for everyone to fit in, regardless of their level of skill or ability. The time I spent in that youth group was a fantastic time for me and I am so happy that I had that experience. I keep in touch with Joy, who remains young at heart and is now living in aged care.

In some of the shows my older brother Gavin and I played *The Entertainer* with him on piano and me on violin. I also played in the youth group band that included a guitarist, saxophone player and a drummer. However, by far the most fun for me was the dancing. Joy's idea of dancing was more a combination of dancing and gymnastics. Because I was quite small, I enthusiastically got the role of being thrown around into the air and spun around majestically. During these dance numbers I

Chapter 3
Childhood and Adolescence

remember being thrown into back flips and being swung around held only by my left foot. I had a fantastic time, and it was exhilarating!

I would open the shows doing the splits in mid-air with one boy holding my left leg out in front of me and another holding my right leg behind me, all to the music *Flash Dance*. This was certainly a spectacular opening and a great way to start our demonstrations, dancing and acts.

This is me, being swung around at Youth Group

Joy was not just a bystander either. She would get involved herself. I remember a fun show where Joy and I did a duet of the old English *Mother's Lament*. The last song on the Cream's album, Disraelia Gears, often known as: *The Baby Went down the Plughole*, with the two of us dressed as babies. It was hilarious and a lot of fun to do.

Joy allowed me to express myself through music and performance. Youth Group became a huge part of my teenage years and helped me to overcome many of my childhood adversities. It bolstered me to push my boundaries and see myself as an individual who could shine within a community of likeminded people.

Whilst at school I grew up in two rural suburbs with a population of around 2000 people. As a young child I had hopes, dreams, and aspirations about being strong and independent, becoming a nurse and helping others through difficult times and meeting the man of my dreams. I was also actively involved in music, tennis, swimming, athletics, ballet, and different forms of dancing. My childhood was robust and many of my dreams became a reality and were the foundations of preparing me to weather the storms of life.

During my teenage years I had established long-term friendships, had a lot of success with sport, furthered my music and had a bunch of great experiences, like the youth group, but adolescence, just like childhood, cannot last for ever. Sooner or later, it comes time to grow up and make your own way in the world. We all do this at different ages and with different levels of ease, but it is a natural part of human life. So, when I had finished school, I was very keen to go to university and get my nursing qualification and start establishing my career and living my own adult life.

During my childhood years we had done so much, and Mum had worked so hard for us to be able to do that. Mum was also Dad's carer and needed to take control of things. Unfortunately this became such a set pattern for her that she had great difficulty when it came time for me to grow up. It was awfully hard for her to loosen the reins and allow me to gracefully navigate the transition from adolescence into independent adulthood.

Chapter 3
Childhood and Adolescence

So, when I finished school, I decided that it was time to move out of home. Because I was accepted into nursing, I had the opportunity to live at the nurses' home attached to the Mater Misericordiae Hospital that was managed by the Sisters of Mercy and near Newcastle university - so that is what I did. I boarded within and it was walking distance to the university which meant that I did not need to buy a car.

Mum was not happy about me moving out of home, so to keep the peace I would go home on the weekends. The good thing about that was it gave me a chance to ride my beloved horse Felicity.

I had always been keen on nursing as a career. I liked the idea of helping others, being able to help people get better and to help make them feel better. I thought that this was a good type of career to follow and was one that could make a difference in people's lives at a time when they needed that help.

When I was in Year 10, each student undertook work experience in their chosen field to see if the job was suitable. I did my work experience at the Mater hospital where I lived three years later, and I loved it. That reinforced my passion and helped me realise that I was on the right career path. At the time of writing this book I am still a registered nurse and still enjoy nursing as a career.

I started my nursing studies at university thirty-four years ago and this is where I met Janice, who remains a close and dear friend who I regard as family. Janice is a beautiful lady, a person with immense knowledge and talent and we connected immediately. Janice welcomes everyone with open arms and excels in bringing out the best in everyone she encounters. Together we have experienced many joyful and meaningful moments. Janice has offered words of encouragement, cheer and support and knows me deeply. I can always be myself around Janice. She is a thoughtful woman who, by her very nature, enhances the lives of others. We have shared many laughs and with every exchange we remain good friends with a special bond. I treasure the time I spend with Janice, and I have many sweet memories of our times together. Janice's friendship is special because she is an amazing person who is treasured, celebrated and quietly thanked for being part of my life.

Janice was a mature age student, and she had a young son, Justin. She would often bring Justin to lectures and we would sit him on our laps. It is hard to believe that he is in his thirties now. It really is incredible how quickly time passes.

There was a lot of study required to become a registered nurse but they were interesting subjects and so I enjoyed the study. My habit of doing whatever study and assignments were required ensured that I did very well.

Because of the amount of study all through the year, the nurses had a traditional way of letting their hair down at the end of each year. They went on a nurses' pub crawl. Not only that, but it was also fancy dress, and the traditional theme was weapons and bondage. I thought it all sounded like a bit of harmless fun, so I was happy to join them.

As I said earlier, I went home on the weekends. So, the first year I took part in this tradition I had to catch a train from home to the pub where we all planned to meet. Here I was dressed in fishnet stockings, short skirt, tight top and outrageous makeup. On the train I ran into a girl I knew from high school and said hello to her, but she totally ignored me. It dawned on me that the way I was dressed must have shocked her, so I tried to explain that I

Chapter 3
Childhood and Adolescence

was on my way to a fancy-dress party, but she did not want to know. I think that she was convinced that I had taken up a different profession and I was on my way to work. The next year I decided not to catch the train!

When I graduated from university I enthusiastically applied for a job and started work at Cessnock District Hospital where I worked full time for four and a half years in various departments. While working there I was also working on a casual basis in the trauma unit at John Hunter Hospital, so I was gaining plenty of professional experience.

At this time, my brother Gavin was working in Germany and his girlfriend was working as a nanny in a castle there. She told him the couple she worked for, a Count and Countess, were wanting a qualified registered nurse to look after their baby and live in the castle with them. Gavin contacted me and asked me if I would like to be a nurse in a castle in Germany. It is not every day that you get the opportunity to live in a castle, so I thought that sounded like something worth doing for a while, so I excitedly said: "Yes, when do I start?"

I am a dual citizen and with my British passport I was quick to jump on a plane for my new adventure. I was twenty-four years old and had never been outside of Australia before, but off I went, on my own, to start my fascinating overseas adventure.

Small Steps
Big Outcomes

Chapter 3
Childhood and Adolescence

- Active lifestyle and having fun.

- Structure movements and actions.

- Celebrate the positives.

- Be both flexible and determined to get what you want out of life.

- Remain ambitious and determined to positively move forward, one small step at a time.

- Consolidate your inner strength.

- Be determined to succeed, move forward and do what it takes.

- Friendships enhance my life.

- Long term effects of doing what is required whenever needed.

- Wanting to facilitate my professional experiences and make a difference in people's lives.

- Last time at home in Australia, fully intact.

- *Vigor in Arduis* … strength in difficulties.

Chapter 4

Exciting Adventures

It is not every day that a twenty-four-year-old woman from country NSW is given the opportunity to work and live in a castle in Germany. But that is exactly the opportunity that I was given and that I accepted. It was a wonderful opportunity and the start of a great adventure.

I arrived in Germany in April 1994. After a few days stay with my brother in Munich, I caught the train the thirty-two kilometres to Grafing station, which is just over two kilometres from Castle Elkofen, or Schloss Elkofen as it is known locally.

This eleventh century gothic castle is ringed by a now dry moat and entry is via an eighteen-metre-high arch. The chapel within the castle, dedicated to St George, contained a winged alter with carved figures. That alter is now kept in the Bavarian National Museum in Munich. The castle has a long and interesting history and has served as a safe refuge for many people throughout the centuries. At the time I worked there it was privately owned by my employers and was both their private home and a conference centre.

Small Steps
Big Outcomes

Schloss Elkofen

The Count and the Countess were welcoming, friendly, and hospitable employers. I had been hired as a qualified registered nurse to look after their newborn baby girl. I originally lived in the main living quarters within the castle but later moved up to the main tower. The working conditions were excellent. I had my meals prepared for me and my laundry done. It really was a great place to work given the pleasant conditions, atmosphere and surroundings. The welcoming family and workers within the castle were very courteous and helped in making my first solo journey overseas not too daunting for me.

I generally worked six days a week and went into the local village or visited my brother Gavin in Munich on my days off. Sometimes I would have a full weekend off and that gave me the chance to travel further afield and see some of the interesting sites.

One of the great things about Europe for a traveller is that everything is so close, and it does not take too long to get to

Chapter 4
Exciting Adventures

another interesting country. During the enjoyable nine months I worked at the castle I got to travel to various parts of Germany, the Czech Republic, France, Austria and Switzerland. Two cities that captivated me were Prague, the most sensationally beautiful city of a hundred spires and Paris, a city of lights, romanticism, and mysteriousness, with a flavour so irresistible that once you experience it you carry around the memories forever.

Here I am climbing the highest mountain in Germany, Zugspitze, in Garmish in 1994.

Of course, if you are living in Germany and it is October then you feel a need to attend the world famous Oktoberfest. Whilst at this festival I ran into a couple who I had trained with at university, and we got to talking about their exciting travels and beneficial working experiences. They were currently living and working in London. They told me that it was an excellent place for gaining career experience and even offered for me to stay at their place initially, while I found a place of my own, if I ever decided to work there myself. After speaking with them I felt that I was missing the clinical side of nursing and decided that I would gain immense knowledge and experience in the London hospitals. Also, after having such wonderful travelling adventures while based in Schloss Elkofen, I imagined that my travelling opportunities would be enhanced if I based myself in London. I had an offer to stay working for the Count and Countess for longer than my original term but after nine months I felt that I wanted more nursing involvement in the hospital system and so off I ventured into another exciting journey to live in London.

As soon as I arrived in London, the largest city in England and the United Kingdom, I joined Nightingale's Nursing Agency and started working as an agency Staff Nurse within numerous hospitals surrounding London. Most of my work was based at the Royal Free Hospital in their busy trauma unit that is situated in the Hampstead area of the London Borough of Camden. I found the experience quite different to what I was accustomed to in Australia, particularly with the effects of the IRA bombings in and around London during 1996, between 9 February and 24 April. I was grateful during this time that I was walking distance from work and did not have to catch the tube train to get there. I got to treat people with a much wider range of injuries than what I would typically see in Australia. I loved working in trauma as you had to think quickly and be at the top of your game, and you could see immediately the benefits the patient was gaining from what you were doing for them. While in London I gained immense professional experience, knowledge and maturity and I found the work diversely enjoyable and personally rewarding.

Another thing that impressed me while working in London hospitals was the high level of team spirit. It has been my observation in some Australian hospitals that often personal politics play a large role at work, but in London every team

Chapter 4
Exciting Adventures

member was given full and genuine respect for the role that they played. It was empowering and inspiring to work in an environment like that and, because the team was such a strong unit, we produced excellent results, which of course gave our patients the best chance of pulling through.

This team spirit even extended to socialising together outside of work and everyone mixed as friends on equal footing, regardless of whether they were doctors, nurses, ambulance drivers or any other team member.

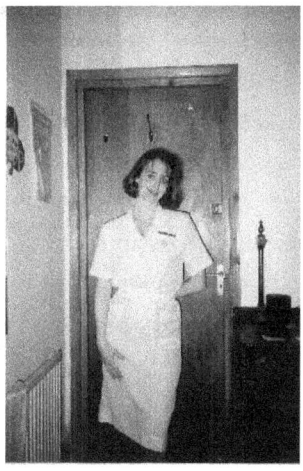

Me, nursing with Nightingale's Nursing Agency in London 1995

I soon targeted the shifts I was accepting so that I only worked in the trauma unit where the dynamic process of patient-centred care was expressed through closeness, immediate therapeutic care and the strongest team spirit. Because of the devastating nature of various injuries and presentations, it was necessary for staff to have excellent working relationships to maintain the positive momentum required. On numerous occasions I would witness immediate results of direct care I had initiated or provided and that was personally rewarding, but the best part of the work for me was the team aspect. We were always working effectively, always focused on doing our best, and on giving the best medical care that we could give. It identified for me the importance of maintaining a high standard of expertise and applying that in such a way as to make the system work for patients and ensure that we achieved the best possible care and associated outcomes.

As well as the required knowledge of the physical side of care, working in trauma also requires a broad understanding of traumatic stress reactions and common responses to traumatic events. I came to really understand how trauma can affect the way that the patient's condition presents itself and, because of this, the way staff engages with that patient. Ultimately, this strongly contributes to the outcome that the patient experiences. I particularly became very aware that trauma affects everyone differently and that some individuals may clearly display symptoms associated with post-traumatic stress disorder (PTSD). I also realised that the impact of trauma can be dangerous, subtle or even outright destructive. I was also aware that the way in which a traumatic event affects an individual depends on many factors, some of which may include personal characteristics of that individual, the type and characteristics of the trauma event and even the circumstances surrounding that trauma.

This experience and knowledge gained while working in a busy trauma unit in a major teaching hospital was further reinforced when, after my own accident, I became a trauma patient myself. Due to the extent of my numerous disabling injuries, my initial dependence on life support, the length of time I remained unconscious and unfortunately contracting meningitis as well, I

Chapter 4
Exciting Adventures

remained in a state of PTSD for months after I regained consciousness.

My dismembered body had received so many and so varied injuries, that it needed to strive extremely hard in an attempt to repair itself as well as it could. I firmly believe that this strength of healing was also strongly influenced by my burning desire to return again to being the Marny that I thought of as me, rather than remaining the unrecognisable Marny that was lying there, beaten up, disfigured and impaired in the hospital bed.

Although I had suffered comprehensive injuries from such a traumatic event, my mindset, from the very beginning, was to concentrate on what I was capable of doing and then to make attempts at improving what was my then current state. I also knew instinctively that I had to remain strong and not be put off by setbacks. I was determined to prevent my attitude from being altered from what I believed it needed to be in order for me to achieve what I wanted to achieve. I will talk more about that in the next chapter.

After having worked for some time for the agency I decided to take the opportunity to join The Royal Free Hospital as a rostered Staff Nurse on a casual basis working in their trauma unit. The advantage of this over the agency work was that I had my shifts rostered in advance, thus giving me financial security but I still kept the flexibility of working on a casual basis. Because I was still a casual, I could ask to be rostered off for periods of time to allow me to travel. I would work full time for approximately four to six weeks to save money and then when I had saved enough, I would go off travelling again.

London is a perfect base for a traveller and, I felt at that time, if you are working there earning at a local pay rate then it was not expensive to live there. From London I travelled through England, Scotland, Wales, Ireland, Turkey, France, Greece, and Italy.

It never ceased to amaze me that in every country I travelled, I would coincidently run into someone I knew from back home in Australia, either from school, university or my hometown. It seems against the laws of probability that I could so often be in the same place at the same time as people that I knew, especially since my hometown was not really a very big place, but time and time again I would hear someone call out: "Marny Cringle, is that you?" And, sure enough there would be someone from home.

One of the trips I made at this time turned out to be a very moving experience that will stay with me for the rest of my life.

April 25th is a special day for Australians. It is a day where, each year, we honour those who have fought in wars and campaigns in order that we can enjoy the freedom that Australians still have right up to the present day. That date in April was chosen because it had particular significance during the first world war when Australian forces were sent to invade the Turkish coast at Gallipoli, with the goal of moving on to capture Constantinople. Terribly, the campaign was doomed to failure right from the start, but the incredible heroism shown by Australian and New Zealand troops during the twelve-month campaign has come to stand for the heroism and sacrifice of Australian soldiers in general. Every year, on April 25, all around Australia, there are dawn services held in remembrance and there is also a dawn service held at Gallipoli, in Turkey.

My most moving experience whilst travelling overseas was when I attended a special anniversary commemoration ceremony to mark the 80th Anniversary of the landing of Australians at Anzac

Chapter 4
Exciting Adventures

Cove in Gallipoli. This landing was part of the amphibious invasion of the Gallipoli Peninsula, and the half-light of dawn was one of the times favoured for launching an attack. I arranged to arrive, prior to attending the dawn service, via boat on Anzac Cove at the similar time and location to where ANZACs first soldiers sailed into their futile battle. I was shocked to see where the soldiers had to alight, in the open with no protection and realised with horror, why this campaign quickly became a stalemate.

A visit to Gallipoli for Anzac Day is a life-changing experience. During the dawn service I was moved to tears as I was again told of the incredible bravery of Australians at the Battle of Lone Pine, which has come to illustrate the courage in the face of the ultimate failure of the Gallipoli campaign. After the dawn service I attended a moving service at the Lone Pine memorial where I planted a tree on the Gallipoli Peninsula, in my name. Lone Pine memorial was surrounded by majestic pine trees encircled by graves and sits poignantly atop Anzac Cove. The memorial housed rows upon rows of grave sites - all adorned with bright coloured flowers or greenery, and it was a bitter-sweet memory to know that this site had been well cared for. It was here that I laid poppies on several graves of soldiers buried at Lone Pine where more than 4,000 soldiers missing in action are also acknowledged at the memorial. Lone Pine displayed the courage, resilience, mateship and sacrifice of Australian soldiers which I feel has helped to forge our country's national character and identity.

I then walked in the footsteps of 50,000 Australians who served at Gallipoli, including the 8000 who never came home. I spent an emotional time amongst the trenches surrounding Lone Pine, Shrapnel Gulley, Monash Gulley, Quin's post, Chunuk Bair,

Small Steps
Big Outcomes

Battleship Hill, Suvla Bay Hill, and The Nek. It was appalling to see and imagine what the ANZACs were faced with and view where they were forced to dig extensive trench and tunnel systems where they had to endure a semi-subterranean existence of cramped and filthy living and working conditions under constant shellfire. I found some shrapnel amongst some of the trenches, and it was alarming to come across remnants of such a brutal time in our history.

Another travel experience that sticks in my mind is when my mother visited me while I was living in London. We shared much delight in travelling together to Paris and throughout the United Kingdom. We went to Barrow-in-Furness (Lake District) where Dad was born and Chepstow (Wales) where Dad was raised.

Chepstow Castle boasts the oldest castle doors in Europe and is situated on a narrow ridge between the limestone river cliff and a valley, known locally as the Del. When we were at Chepstow Mum and I contacted Dad, who was being cared for in a respite service, via telephone and he mentioned to look for a bridge in the grounds of the castle. When at Chepstow Castle we could not see a bridge but when we asked the castle guard at the gate, he did mention that there was a dense area that was out of bounds, and it is most likely in that area. We decided that the out of bounds area was safe, and we really wanted to find that bridge, so we ventured in and, sure enough, found the bridge that Dad was talking about.

When I was a young child, Dad would often sing a song to my brothers and I that he used to sing when he was young, on his adventures throughout the forest surrounding Chepstow Castle. The only words I can remember Dad singing now are: '...we are the mystery riders we come from near and far...' I have since

Chapter 4
Exciting Adventures

found out that the song was the theme song to a series of movies that were very popular when Dad was a boy. When we were in Chepstow and rang Dad, we sang him the part of the song that we knew, and it is a great memory to have. Both Mum and Dad have passed now, and I see myself as incredibly lucky to have travelled, with Mum, to the place of Dad's birth and childhood.

This is me with a Guard at the front of Chepstow Castle on 9.10.95

My brother Gavin was the one who told me about the opportunity to work overseas in Germany and so it was only fitting that I also had the chance to do some travelling with him while I was living in Germany.

I had a spectacular time with Gavin when I lived in Germany. From Munich we drove to and then around Switzerland with its mountainous countryside and high peaks of the Alps.

We stayed in Zermatt in southern Switzerland which is a renowned mountain resort that lies beneath the iconic Matterhorn peak. I was tempted by a charming young man to stay there and work but with reluctance turned down the opportunity and headed back to Germany.

Small Steps
Big Outcomes

When I was living in London Gavin was still based in Munich. Just prior to his return home to Australia he visited me with his son Edan and they stayed for six days. I showed them a few of the sights of London and introduced Gavin to some of my friends. Who would have guessed that just over two months later he would again come to London to accompany my mother to be at my side for a vastly different reason? But more of that later.

Violin playing is my passion and I feel as though it has been a part of me since I was born. Playing the violin offers me an emotional outlet and provides me with an opportunity to release my feelings.

Whilst travelling I was missing the physical and mental challenges that violin playing provides, along with the expression of raw emotion. I get so much joy and personal satisfaction from playing my violin and was determined to purchase a violin overseas to accompany my adventures and to enhance my musical experiences.

While living in London I joined the Fulham Symphony Orchestra (FSO), and this brought more depth and passion into my violin playing and a chance to experience a side of London that was truly inspiring. I had played violin in various orchestras ever since I was in high school and so it was great to be playing with an orchestra again, this time in London. It reminds me of how universal music is and how great it is to be able to play wonderful music and share that playing with other musicians, regardless of where you are in the world.

The FSO was a high standard orchestra that always played an interesting and challenging classical repertoire. The orchestra consisted of a very friendly bunch of people who really saw each member as a valuable team member, and everyone was

Chapter 4
Exciting Adventures

comfortable mixing with everyone else. Back in Australia I had sometimes experienced orchestras where members of each section would mainly only talk to others from the same section, but with the FSO there was none of that and it was a pleasure to play in that orchestra.

At my first night of rehearsal with them they made me feel very welcome. An elderly member of the orchestra, Herman, found out that I had caught a couple of tube trains to get there and that I lived in the same suburb as he did. Herman then stopped out the front of where I was living and took me to and from rehearsals each week, and that really made me feel part of the team straight away.

London was not all travel, music and work, there were also other exhilarating adventures!

As I have said before there was good camaraderie in our Accident and Emergency (A & E) trauma unit, and we all got along very well with the regular crew from the London Ambulance Service (LAS) who frequented our unit. I became friends with a few paramedics, who asked me to join them in a fundraising activity. A few of us travelled in an ambulance to an area that was about six and a half hours out of London, Peterborough Parachute Centre, to do a parachute training course prior to jumping out of a plane for a dramatic parachute descent. This was only four months before my accident. I jumped out of a plane that did not have a door!

Prior to jumping out of the plane and parachuting we learnt how to crash into buildings, plummet through trees, drag along roof tops and land into water, hoping of course that we would not have to put any of that training into practice. I was sore from training, and I did not know why I was doing this stupid act. I thought I must have been crazy for wanting to jump out of a plane, all in aid for cancer research … mad!!

On the big day I was a little nervous, especially when I packed my own parachute. We had our final briefing from the instructor before we geared up on the airfield. I was all fired up and ready to go but then we were told that the wind was too high for us to jump, so we had to unload our parachutes. The wind was seventeen knots, and we were told that we could only jump when it was ten knots or less. At 12pm the winds were still up, and I was not impressed as it was looking like we would not be able to jump after all. At 2pm people started leaving for home, but I refused to go back to London unless I was told that the jump was being cancelled. According to what I was told the wind always drops between 5 - 6 pm and so I still held high hope that the jump was just being delayed and that we would get to do it sooner or later.

At 4pm the wind was still increasing, and everyone was feeling at an all-time low, our spirits had been well and truly dampened. I was thinking that it would be extremely disappointing to go home to London without jumping, especially with my sore muscles reminding me of all the training and preparation that I had done just so that I could do the jump.

I do not know why, but I phoned Mum to tell her where I was and what I was doing. After I phoned her, she was very worried so I told her I would phone her again, after I had parachuted, to tell her about my jump.

Shortly after 4pm we got the go ahead to jump. Now that it was really going to happen, I was more nervous than I had been earlier in the day, so much so that I almost chickened out. I was told that I would be the first person to jump and that meant that

Chapter 4
Exciting Adventures

I had to sit in the doorway of the plane that did not have a door. I can tell you that I was appropriately nervous about sitting there. When the plane took off, and the whole time it was climbing, all I could think about was: "What if I fall out of the plane before we get high enough for my parachute to work?" But luckily that did not happen. When we reached the height to jump it was time to pluck up my courage again and just do it. While jumping out of the plane I somehow caught my pack on the doorway, and I summersaulted out of the plane!

It was supposed to be a straightforward thing to jump out of the plane, but here I was tumbling head over heels and not knowing which way was up or down. I was petrified and thought that I was going to die for certain. I remember thinking that I must have rung Mum because I somehow subconsciously knew that I was soon going to die. I was also thinking about how much it was going to hurt when I hit the ground with my parachute still closed.

However, about five exceptionally long seconds later my canopy opened, and I was saved... but was I? With horror I realised that I had a twist in my line, which meant I was out of control. I was terrified again! Thankfully, I managed to frantically kick out the twist, grab my toggles, and finally I had control of the parachute. Once I was in control, everything changed. I was captivated by the ease at which I was floating through the sky, and I was awestruck by the beautifully landscaped scenery below me.

I could not see the drop zone but that was not worrying me, I had a spectacular view, so I was enjoying it. I ran with the wind for a short while before holding and slowly drifted back. I was so excited when I landed as somehow, I did manage to land in the drop zone, even though I landed with more of a thud than I expected, and I jarred my back. It is a testament to the quality of the instructor we had during training because as soon as I hit the hard ground that training kicked in and I immediately jumped up and ran around my parachute before the wind could get hold of it and drag me along. The jump was a euphoric and exhilarating experience where words cannot justly explain the combination of both relief and excitement that I felt.

I was on such a high after I parachuted that I just wanted to celebrate, but training kicked in again and I dutifully went to the packing shed to repack the parachute first. Everyone was feeling tremendous and had huge cheesy grins. It really had been a magnificent experience, and one that I will always remember for the rest of my life.

It was here at Peterborough Parachute Centre in the United Kingdom that I had another of those coincidences that seem to defy expectations. Here at the parachute centre, I was introduced to the world champion parachute instructor, who by the way is in a wheelchair, and I find out that he is based in an area in the Hunter Valley vineyards, just a short drive from where I lived and grew up in Australia. I was always happy when I met with someone I either knew or lived near me in Australia when I was in foreign land as we shared something in common and had some interesting conversations.

After this amazing parachuting experience we returned to London to release some of our excitement there. I then remembered to phone Mum and I also called a couple of my friends in London, full of screaming joy and excitement. I was still euphoric, yet totally exhausted, when I went to bed on that evening of 26 July 1996. I was truly living a great life that was filled with many unique adventures and good times.

Chapter 4
Exciting Adventures

You often hear it said that chance meetings can change a person's life forever. On the 6 October 1996 I had arranged to meet a friend at Heathrow airport as she had just returned to London after a hectic adventure abroad. After we got her things back to her flat, we headed into the Outback, which was a lively Australian pub in London's West End. As soon as I walked inside, I ran into some friends I knew from my hometown. Meeting up with these people in London profoundly changed the course of my life!

One of my friends, Paul, introduced me to his sweet and bubbly girlfriend Kim, who has since become his wife, and we clicked immediately. On my return to Australia after my accident this beautiful lady has continued to enrich my life, she has provided me with ongoing support and has become a dear friend who has left a footprint in my heart and makes the world around her special by simply being in it.

Kim is like an angel without wings, who brightens my day in a variety of wonderful magical ways whenever I see her or speak with her over the phone. Kim is an incredibly special lady who gives others a reason to smile and deserves only the best in return. I sincerely hope that the happiness Kim gives away will come back to warm her for the remainder of her days.

Living in London was a time of my life where everything was going along so well for me. I was 26 years old and felt that I had the world at my feet. I was happily working in my chosen career and gaining valuable experience with an exceptional team of colleagues. I was traveling to all the places I wanted to visit. I had friends around me. I was having fun playing sport and keeping fit. I was playing violin in a great orchestra, and I was having many great adventures, including parachuting. In fact, by the age of twenty-six years, life was simply perfect. I had everything I wanted, I was living on purpose and there was nothing I felt I could not achieve.

I had the opportunity, and the plan, to stay in London for another eighteen months to finish my travels before saving money and returning to Australia to buy my own house and settle down. My life was going along so well, and my future looked like it was right on track to be exactly what I had hoped it would be. I never guessed that just around the corner fate would pull the rug out from under me and throw me challenges that I would have to battle with for many years to come.

Chapter 4
Exciting Adventures

- High level of team spirit is empowering and produces excellent results.

- Maintaining and delivering a high standard of expertise to achieve desired outcome.

- The impact of trauma affects everyone differently.

- Adopting a mindset to concentrate on capabilities and not be put off by setbacks.

- Could music be the medicine for life?

- Friends can leave a footprint in your heart.

- Circumstances can certainly impact and alter your life.

Chapter 5

Uncertain Future

DEATH DEFYING INCIDENT

I have already mentioned that meeting Kim that first time in London was a life changing event because we ended up becoming, and remaining, such good friends and she has always been a great friend and supportive during both the good times and the tough times after my accident. However, there is more to tell about the story of that day.

Amongst the group of Australians that I ran into on 6 October 1996 was another friend from my hometown, a young man named David who is a very sweet and charming gentleman. Over the next few weeks we began spending some time together as he made me laugh, made me feel good within myself and he treated me with tenderness. On 5 November I flew into Rome and travelled around Italy on my own for a couple of weeks. Absence did make the heart grow fonder and on 11 November, David accepted a reverse charge call from me while I was in Florence so I could let him know that I was thinking of him and that everything was going well. When I returned to Heathrow airport from Rome, it was the first time anyone had been waiting for me at the airport and it was a pleasure to see David again.

The Tube is a slang name for the London Underground, because some of the tunnel lines are like that of round tubes running through the ground. The London Underground, better known as the Tube, has eleven lines, serves two hundred and seventy stations, covers over four hundred and eight kilometres of track, transports up to five million passenger journeys daily and can travel speeds up to one hundred kilometres an hour.

A friend of a friend was arranging a get together, because she was supposedly going back home to South Africa, (I was later told she had no intentions of going back home, it was just a good excuse to organise a get together). Had I of known this I certainly would not have made the effort to go. Regardless, David and I went to the assumed farewell together. It was Sunday night, the 1st of December 1996, a date I will never forget!

The meeting with my friends was originally planned for lunch time and David came over to my place in the morning. It was only about a ten-minute tube ride to get to where we had to be, and we were about to leave when I received a phone call to ask if we could go to their place in the early evening. I did not mind as there was a sense of excitement in the air because I was happy with the thought of having someone with me to celebrate my birthday and Christmas this year. I did not particularly like the time we were to meet up as it was the first day of winter which is the coldest month in London where temperatures are often at freezing point. The weather in London is very erratic and the winters are usually wet and windy so when we left my flat, I automatically headed out with my long thick winter coat down to my ankles to ensure I kept warm and to protect me from unexpected weather conditions. When we arrived, we were welcomed and shared some happy memories.

We had only been at Willesden Green a short while when David mentioned he was tired and needed to leave as it would take him over an hour to get home to where he was living, and he had to work the next day. I was not working the next day so I

Chapter 5
Uncertain Future

accompanied David as he would be travelling alone from Northwest London to Southwest London via three tube lines and I had previously made this trip several times to visit David or travel to orchestra rehearsal and knew exactly where to go. We said our farewells to those at the so-called farewell, got on the train on the Jubilee line and travelled from Willesden Green to Green Park tube station to transfer onto another tube and it was here that my horrific accident occurred. We had to catch two trains home to where David was living, trains that I would not have otherwise caught, and it was on the change-over platform at Green Park tube station that I had my terrible accident.

I know logically that David was not to blame for my accident, but humans are not always logical creatures. I admit that there have been times when I thought that if I had never run into David while living in London then I would never have had the accident. I also know that the accident made a terrible impact on his life too. David was not hit by the train, and he was not looking in my direction when the accident occurred. But he witnessed the immediate result of the young woman he was with, mangled beyond recognition, and he heard my blood curdling screams when I was hit by the unstoppable tube train made of thick welded steel weighing up to one hundred and sixty-seven ton. That is a terrible experience that must be extremely hard to forget, so I am sure that he too has had times when he wished we had never run into one another again in London. If that has been the case with him then I can fully understand. Ultimately, I am responsible for my own life.

However, David saved my life that night, and I am eternally grateful for his heroic acts! After David had heard my shocking screams there was silence, and when the tube train departed from the platform, he witnessed the horrific sight of my bloodied and mutilated body lying unconscious on the tube line. David then realised that it was only one minute before the next train was due to arrive exactly where I was lying unconscious. It must have been a horrific sight for him to see me lying there with parts of my brain on the tube line, several areas of my brain exposed and most of the bones in my skull shattered and embedded within the remaining areas of my brain, my left leg amputated with blood spurting out everywhere, my right leg semidetached and only just still connected to my dismembered body, and numerous other injuries, some of which could not be seen. But he put his own life at risk and courageously jumped down to get me off the tracks before the next train arrived. So ultimately, he saved my life, and I will forever be thankful that he was there to save me! If it were not for David's selfless act to get me off the tracks, I would not be alive today because I would not have survived long enough to be given an opportunity to recover from my injuries. Thankfully, I am alive today, but only because the brave, heroic David acted quickly and prevented my already distorted body from being hit by another train, which certainly would have been the death blow, with no chance of recovery.

I truly wish that I never had that accident, but unfortunately, wishes cannot change the past. What has already happened has happened and must be accepted. Just one minute, or even a second sometimes, can change the course of your life forever. I had never planned to be there on that platform at that exact time, but somehow circumstances ensured that I was, and my life was changed forever as a result.

Something that I have learned from my accident is that your life can be totally altered in such an unexpected way by chance events, and you can be thrown into a completely new and unexpected direction. This consequently opens up a whole new

Chapter 5
Uncertain Future

dimension within yourself that you were not aware of or knew existed. You will then be forced to reassess everything in an extremely different way, and you may even be required to face the most complicated and challenging time of your life. If that ever happens to you, as it did to me, it will change you permanently! However, if you believe in the strength of the human spirit, then that belief may enable you to set and achieve new goals and give you the strength to keep going even when the going gets tough.

I would never have guessed that I had it in me to find a way to cope with a situation like that. But we do not know what is possible until we are put under the right amount of pressure. Just like me, you may also think that you could not move forward after something like that, but the reality is that there is no telling what hidden strengths are inside you, just waiting to jump into action when the need is great enough.

My life had changed direction with that accident and there was no escaping that, but, once the initial shock had subsided enough, I realised that I had to remain positive. One thing I knew for certain was that however I chose to view my new circumstances; it was up to me to make the most of them.

I do not know the full details of how my accident happened as I have no conscious memory of it, but from what I have been told the most likely thing that happened was that my long coat was somehow caught on a moving train, which then dragged me along for approximately sixty metres. When the train went through the tunnel at the end of the platform I was slammed against the wall, and this is when my leg was amputated. I feel that if there was no tunnel for the train to go through, I would have been dragged considerably further and probably met with an unavoidable death.

There was a security camera on the platform, but when I tried later to track it down, I was told that the footage was destroyed and so I have never had the opportunity to watch it. Nevertheless, being run over by a train has changed my life dramatically, and I have come to accept that and am grateful to be alive and living independently. I do not dwell on how my accident happened or the what-ifs. I channel my energy and focus into making the most of my life.

To be hit by a train in the London underground is more common than most people realise, but very rarely does someone survive. As mentioned previously, at that time, I was working as a registered nurse in one of the London trauma units and while working there I witnessed a number of trauma cases who were train accident victims, but unfortunately they all died as a result of their accident.

When you read the extent of my injuries it might help you to understand just why it is so rare to survive such an accident.

My most obvious injury is where my left leg was immediately ripped off by the train. However, my most severe injury is fortunately not obvious today and that is my skull was completely smashed. In fact, one of the doctors likened it to an eggshell after it had been dropped from the top of a ten-storey building. I was told that I had so many fractures in my skull that the doctors were unable to count them all, and part of my skull was missing altogether leaving my brain exposed in several areas, mainly in the right parietal region.

Chapter 5
Uncertain Future

When my skull was being smashed, several parts of my brain were also ripped out and are gone forever, and bones from my smashed skull were embedded in the remaining areas of my exposed brain causing further damage.

In addition to these brain injuries, my eyes were completely knocked out of their sockets and were hanging out of my head and my spine was severely broken in five places. I also had multiple rib fractures and both of my lungs had collapsed and were filled with blood. There were many other debilitating injuries too numerous to mention in detail, but the train left me lying on the tracks, unconscious with blood gushing out of me, and only one minute before the next train was due to arrive exactly where I was lying. I certainly would not have survived if I were hit by another train but due to David's immediate actions, strength, courage and caution he somehow lifted my mangled and bloodied body off the tube line and out of harm's way or certain death.

THE EDGE BETWEEN LIFE AND DEATH

An ambulance arrived shortly after David somehow lifted me back onto the hard-cold platform and I was taken to hospital, even though they did not expect me to survive the trip. I was not aware at the time of course, because I was unconscious, but I found out later that the paramedics were ones that I knew through A & E at the Royal Free Hospital where I worked at that time. This time though I was not the nurse waiting to help a trauma patient in need, I was the trauma patient being rushed into emergency. When I arrived at the hospital, I was still unconscious and remained in a coma for about a week and was immediately placed on life support for about a week also.

In addition to the above-mentioned injuries, my whole left side was paralysed, and my right leg had come close to being ripped off as well by the train. It was so gravely injured that the doctors were seriously considering whether it may need to be surgically amputated, which would have left me with no legs at all. Fortunately for me I got to keep my right leg and I am incredibly grateful for that. To top off my list of injuries, I also contracted a life-threatening illness, meningitis. Things were not looking good for me during that stage. It was when I contracted meningitis and given my extensive brain injuries, it was suggested that my life support be turned off as they thought I would have no quality of life IF I ever came out of my coma.

I was so badly smashed up in the accident that when I was lying unconscious in my hospital bed, I was totally unrecognisable. When Mum arrived at the Intensive Care Unit (ICU) from Australia, because of the condition I was in, she placed a photograph of me above my bedhead so that the people caring for me would remember to treat me as a living person and not just a body waiting to die. I was with two friends in the photograph, and everyone who looked at the photograph, and then looked at me lying in the bed, would have to ask Mum: "Which one in that photo is Marny?"

Mum was there at the hospital because the doctors had telephoned her when they initially received me at the hospital following a trauma call. When I arrived at the hospital, my brain was exposed, and my skull was so fragile I needed urgent lifesaving surgeries. I was in a critical state. Before I could be operated on, they had to contact my next of kin, my mother in

Chapter 5
Uncertain Future

Australia, for her permission to perform my surgeries. When the trauma surgeon spoke to Mum to gain her consent, he also left her with a dose of reality – not to expect miracles because the most likely outcome is that she would be bringing me home in a body bag.

After this distressing phone call Mum immediately arranged for my father to be cared for and within roughly thirty-six hours had flown to London from Australia with my older brother, Gavin, to be with me in hospital. My younger brother, Jason, chose to move from where he was renting in Sydney back to our family home so that he could help my uncle care for my father.

Looking back now I can really feel for Mum and how emotionally stressful it must have been for her to get that news. She herself had just gotten out of hospital the previous evening after a Christmas beetle had lodged itself in her ear, so I can imagine she was not feeling 100% either. She had already had her whole life changed twenty-five years earlier, when Dad had his accident, and she was still his constant carer, and then, out of the blue, her perfectly healthy daughter is involved in a very serious accident and her prospect of survival is slim. At that time, I was still balancing on the knife's edge between life and death and the doctors were not giving her any good news as to which side of that knife I was likely to end up. She must have wondered why she was being thrown into this situation again, but in any case, she rushed straight over to London to be with me and to make sure that I was getting the best treatment and care. To her great credit, and testament to her emotional courage and personal strength, Mum remained at my side for months, along with my brother, and impacted greatly on the quality of care I received.

Small Steps
Big Outcomes

I not only had the tremendous support of my mother and brother, but I also had amazing support from my generous local community back home in Australia who rallied around immensely which resulted in support nationwide. When I came out of my coma, I was told by Mum of the extent to which my local community of Maitland was rallying to support me. Friends of my mother phoned her at the hospital in London to ask how she would feel if they organised a fundraiser on my behalf. The appeal was launched the week before Christmas and, despite the pressures that arise at this time of year, the donations were overwhelming.

My dear friends within the Maitland community held a variety of benefit days and nights and other activities to raise funds to help me. The movie, Evita, was one particular fundraiser. As she delivered a passenger to the event, a lady taxi driver jumped out of her taxi, ran over to where tickets were being sold and said: "I know what this is for and I am not going to the movie, here is some money for the cause," before running back to her taxi. The taxi driver is one example of how people responded to the appeal. It was an incredible effort by a whole community working together because they understood my situation and that I needed help and support, and they showed it immensely! Even when the appeal opened the week of Christmas, despite the timing of this appeal, money was donated in the first three days. Usually, a time when cash is scarce but for this community it was a true Christmas of giving to others.

I find it an incredibly moving experience to receive the generosity and support from a large percentage of people within the community of Maitland and some support from various communities within Australia and New Zealand. Their efforts made a considerable difference to me returning home and

Chapter 5
Uncertain Future

having funds available to meet my immediate needs. I do not know how I could have gotten through those challenges without the help and support they gave. Knowing that my hometown had responded so generously to help me, in a time of great need, really helped to give me the strength and determination that I needed to conquer my injuries and I will always be incredibly grateful to them.

That is a whole other story that I will go into later but first things first. So back to what was happening in London.

After Mum's consent was given for my surgeries to proceed in London, I was rushed into the operating theatre where they worked on me for around four hours. They worked to refashion the traumatic amputation of my left leg, they also worked on my right leg in an attempt to save it from being surgically amputated, and they did other necessary procedures required in order to maximise my chances of remaining alive.

Half an hour after coming out of the operating theatre I was transferred to another hospital, Queen Square, the National Hospital for Neurology and Neurosurgery, for emergency brain surgery. It had been assessed that I had a high chance of dying during the transfer, more than 50%, but they judged it to be a near certainty that I would die if I did not get the surgery, so they had to pick what they considered as the better of the two bad options.

Neurosurgery was required to elevate bone fragments from the depressed compound fractures that were pressing into my brain. Surgical reconstruction was performed in the areas through which my brain was exposed, mainly in the right parietal region, and they also had to stem the bleeding that was occurring in that area of my brain.

Small Steps
Big Outcomes

Thankfully, the surgeries were a great success. They not only saved my life, but they also did a great job putting all the pieces back together. I was told recently by my dear friend Kim that when she first saw me back in Australia, months after the accident, my forehead still looked like a jigsaw puzzle. Now, remarkably, my forehead is totally normal again and you would never even guess that it had been damaged to the horrific extent it had been.

After three days in Queens Square Hospital, during which time Mum and Gavin arrived from Australia, I was transferred back to the original hospital to remain there until I had recovered sufficiently to be transferred back to Australia for long-term rehabilitation. For this transfer I was given a 50% chance of survival, but it was necessary for my recovery if I were to survive.

At one point in time, I am certain I was still unconscious as it felt like I was floating in a black void. I could not hear anything. I could not see anything. I could not smell anything. But I could certainly feel something. It was very soothing and comforting. Suspended in blackness, it was instinctively familiar, and a spark of realisation hit me. I wore my hair long on the days I was not working. In my comatose state, I just knew those reassuring fingers were not trailing through my long hair. This naked touch was different. Through the blackness, the sensation of someone touching my naked scalp was amazingly sharp in my mind. Skin on skin. As I lay attuning my connection to this person, who I now know was my mother, my soul was consoled with a single maternal touch.

A subtle touch changed my focus from my inner turmoil that my body, struggling to repair its damaged self, had placed upon my mind. Physically, the bandages had been removed to reveal the

Chapter 5
Uncertain Future

extent of my injury to my family. The red and inflamed scalp covering what was left of my remaining skull, was held together with staples.

About a week later I finally regained consciousness, but I was still very vague and have virtually no memories of those first few days. However, I do remember a time when I was just lying in the bed: I did not understand what was happening to me and why I was in the position I was in. It was as though I was watching a silent 3D movie. I could not move or say anything. I could only look straight ahead, which was up to the ceiling. I was not aware of the severity of my situation or that I was on the brink of death. But I knew that something radical had happened and I could not understand why I was not able to move or do anything. I was so overwhelmed by the situation I was in! I could not move as I had two chest drains on either side as both of my lungs had collapsed, tubes and lines were connected to me in several places. I was paralysed down my left side, had broken my back in five places – one break being a quarter of a millimetre from making me a paraplegic – and my right leg was being held together as they were trying to save it and not have to surgically amputate.

Medical records show that I did start to say a few words over those initial few days of consciousness, but it was simply repeating things said to me rather than initiating my own words. It was also noted in the record that I appeared to be depressed and withdrawn. Even though I was now semi-conscious I spent most of my time asleep. Apparently, some days I would repeat a few words said to me and even mumble some incoherent words of my own, but other days I made no attempt to speak at all.

My mother and brother spent as much time as they could with me in the hospital, even while I was still unconscious. David also spent a lot of time there supporting me - even though it took a great emotional toll on him and some days it was just too upsetting for him to come to the hospital. I am grateful to the three of them for supporting me through those tough times and I also empathise with them for the emotional stress it must have put them through.

On the 9th of December, eight days after being hit by the train, I turned twenty-seven years of age, but it was not something to celebrate. The future still looked very bleak for me at that stage.

What memories I do have from those early times (frustration at not being able to do anything, frustration at how people treated me, only having enough energy to listen to the conversations around me or look at those at my bedside) makes me realise that I had more awareness than anyone thought I had. It was just that my body needed a lot of rest in order to go about its self-repair work. My brain particularly needed rest as it had a massive amount of repairing to do and that left very little energy or focus to give to others. I appreciated the support around me, but I just had no energy to interact much with them.

I do not remember the time I regained consciousness. My first conscious memories of this time are thinking about what was happening to me and of being extremely disappointed at having to be totally dependent on others.

Waking up from the coma I had been in was a defining moment. Once I understood how bad my situation was and how mangled my body and brain were, I had two options. I could give up on life and surrender to adversity or fight with everything in me and create my best life.

Chapter 5
Uncertain Future

My outlook, despite how overwhelmed I was by my predicament, was that if I survived today, tomorrow would come. One step at a time.

I had always been a very independent person by nature, even from childhood, and the concept of depending on others did not sit well with me at all. I had often worked towards achieving something and very soon I started internally setting my own goals and the first goal I set was to regain my independence.

It may surprise you, but I do not remember when I first became aware that I had lost my left leg. At the time of writing this memoir, it has been twenty-five years since the accident, so I have been living as an amputee for a long time now. Also, it is normal after a very traumatic event, and particularly after massive brain injury, that there is a period of post-traumatic amnesia (PTA) and then a further period when the memories are sketchy. Medical reports covering that early period do not specifically note my initial reaction to discovering that I was an amputee and they certainly do not document when I first realised my left leg was gone.

You may not know it, but most amputees still feel, at times, their missing limb as if it is still there. I could still feel the toes of my left foot until very recently and I still, to this very day, get severe phantom limb pain in my missing left leg.

As far as my initial emotional reaction to limb loss, I have been told of an incident shortly after I had regained consciousness when a doctor came in and just threw back my blankets exposing that my leg was missing. This was apparently the first time anyone had openly addressed my amputation while I was conscious, and I am told that I gave him the dirtiest of looks and held my intent gaze on him for a while. My medical report also

Small Steps
Big Outcomes

notes that there were days when I would totally deny having lost a leg. One time, while left unattended, I tried to get out of bed on my own, apparently not realising that I had a missing leg, and I was later found lying on the floor!

It is a very traumatic event to lose a limb and particularly to lose a leg when I had always been such an active sportswoman and dancer. Luckily for me, it has always been my personality that when there are circumstances that cannot be changed, I quickly accept that it is better to come to grips with that reality and to focus on ways to make the best of the situation. That is probably something I learned from watching the way Mum coped with her situation throughout the years after Dad's accident.

Around the time that I set my goal to become independent again I also set a goal that I would get a prosthetic leg that would enable me to walk on two legs again. I also set a sub-goal that, when it came time to be discharged from hospital, I would walk out the hospital on two legs.

I did achieve my goal of walking on two legs again, but it happened in two stages separated by many years and much physical and emotional pain and suffering. But at the time I set my initial walking goal I did not have a clue about all those challenges that I would have to face over the coming years.

Before I could achieve my two major goals, namely regaining independence and walking on two legs again, I had to focus on gaining small wins as bit by bit I started to take back control of my body and brain. Being able to sit up on my own was one of those wins. On the 13th of December I could, for the first time sit up in bed. I needed assistance to get into the sitting position, but once sitting I could stay there briefly, although I fatigued quickly and soon became very unstable and lost control of my head and

Chapter 5
Uncertain Future

trunk. It was hard emotionally and physically, and it was confronting because I was not able to do what my mind wanted me to do. But at the same time, sitting up was a small win just the same and in the physical condition I was in I had to celebrate any small gain because I was not able to do anything on my own. At that point I was too weak to speak and was only capable of watching what was going on around me. But even in the state I was in, I was determined to be independent again. So, I had to be patient and persist in moving forward just one small step at a time and I took encouragement from every small improvement I made. I wanted to be independent, and I wanted to walk again one day.

I soon realised that I needed to push myself for the outcome of my efforts would impact on my life significantly. There was no time for regrets or later thinking I should have tried harder. My left side was paralysed and even though I was in a fragile state and very weak, I focused on my strengths and worked extremely hard at what was required and improve my capabilities. I knew I had a long road ahead of me and it was so important for me to acknowledge any improvement I made and celebrate small wins to keep me motivated throughout a time in my life that was very daunting. As with many other times in my life, I told myself that in everything I can't do there is a CAN which led to me approaching my struggles with the mindset of ...

There is a **CAN** in every can't.

About six weeks later I managed to drink and eat a little although I was still being primarily tube fed. Activities and skills that I had always taken for granted, because I had been doing them since I was a baby, now presented a challenge and had to be relearned and remastered.

Small Steps
Big Outcomes

The most difficult aspect of the task of recovering from my devastating injuries is the extreme frustration that was ever present. Internally I wanted to be myself again and get on with my life, however, my body did not remember how to follow my commands and even my brain had lost the skill to send the right signals to make my body fall into line.

All this physical and mental effort of trying to repair my body and brain and to recover some of my basic, essential skills, took its toll on me and resulted in extreme fatigue. I just had to sleep and sleep and then sleep some more to muster enough energy again to do the simplest of things.

Throughout this I appreciated the support I was getting from those around me, but I did not have the energy or ability to thank them at that time. All the energy I could muster was required just to keep living and keep moving slowly forward a tiny bit at a time.

As well as being physically exhausting it was also emotionally exhausting to have to relearn those basic skills again. There were days when I felt down and saw all the difficulties, but underneath it all, I still had a strong belief that I would recover and that I would live a normal life again. It was those hopes and trust in myself, that gave me the strength to keep going.

I was aware that realistically not everything was possible. I felt that when I was thrown into the deep end of life, my attitudes were more important than the mere facts. If I visualised my goals, and believed that they would occur, then this would help to motivate me to do what it took to accomplish those goals and enjoy the benefits that resulted from achieving them. Of course, there were lots of downs and at times it all seemed too much, but I needed to find a way to work through those feelings and convince myself to think positively again. I found it to be a

Chapter 5
Uncertain Future

constant battle where I would wrestle with my emotions whenever they were negative and do my best to push them into the positive. It was mind over matter, one step at a time, realising that things do not happen straight away and persistence and belief in what I was capable of. I honestly believe that, in the end, the only limitations are the ones you set yourself. If I knew that I had done my best, then I could accept whatever outcome and try to make the most of my given situation!

On the 17th of December, I was moved from the ICU to the Neurological and Stroke Ward. This turned out to be a major factor in relation to the care I was receiving.

Before you read my comments on the standard of care I received in this ward, it is important to remember that as soon as I finished high school, some ten years before my accident, I went immediately to university to study nursing and then worked as a registered nurse in Australia, Germany and in London. At the time of writing this memoir I am still working as a registered nurse. I believe that to be a nurse is a very responsible position and should only be taken on by those who are committed to doing the best job they can possibly do and be an advocate for their patients.

Being a registered nurse myself for many years I feel that I am professionally qualified to judge the difference between good nursing and bad or unacceptable nursing behaviours. The nurses who cared for me whilst I was in the ICU were exceptionally good. However, when I was discharged from ICU and was being cared for in the Neurological and Stroke Ward it is my opinion that some of the nurses working there, at that point in time, were neglectful, inadequate, unprofessional and, at times, tended to ignore the needs of their patients. I do not like to criticise people from my own profession, but I really felt that those particular nurses did not care enough, often lacked consideration and did not know how to deal with someone in my condition or have the patient's best interest at heart.

The left side of my body was paralysed, and I was not to weight bear as they were trying to avoid surgical amputation of my right leg. I had staples and clips holding my leg together. I had foot drop due to nerve damage and paralysis of my foot muscles and I did not have the physical strength or coordination to be able to stand.

Despite the directions the nurses were given and the importance of how much my life would be affected if I lost both of my legs, the nurses would just come in, disregard my injuries and capabilities, and get me to transfer, instead of lifting me. This meant that I was weight bearing during the transfer on my right leg that was not functioning, while my left side was still paralysed. Mum would then have to remind the nurses that I was not to weight bear, and one reply was: "Well, I can't lift her, I'm pregnant." If she was pregnant, why did she agree to care for someone like me who needed lifting and required full assistance with all aspects of care? Why did she not arrange for another capable staff member to lift and assist me, as requested by the medical experts, to avoid further deterioration of my fragile state.

On occasions, Mum and Gavin would notice a lump had appeared on my face or head overnight. I had to be observed constantly because I was still vague at the time due to my brain injuries, and I would sometimes attempt to get out of bed myself and would fall. Unfortunately, at times, staff would leave me alone for too long and things would happen. Mum would notice

Chapter 5
Uncertain Future

new bumps and bruises on my head or face that have permanently remained. Mum and Gavin then decided to stay with me on a twenty-four-hour basis, believing this would better meet my needs. There were many other incidents with inadequate nursing care in the hospital and therefore my mother organised for an agency nurse to look after me one-on-one as my movements were unpredictable and I needed to be monitored closely to prevent further injuries. Mum thought she was a godsend.

I did receive the utmost care and treatment from my doctors but, unfortunately, they often underestimated me and were all extremely doubtful of my chances of recovery, particularly regarding my brain injuries.

In fairness, the principal hospital staff were focused on the immediate problems of keeping me alive and providing means for the best recovery possible. I am incredibly grateful for their efforts in that regard. However, a side effect of being so focused on those immediate needs was that they overlooked some diagnostic procedures. Weeks after my accident, Mum noticed some lumps in my lower back, and by observing my movement and things I was doing, thought that there may be something wrong with my back. She then requested that I have a back X-ray that subsequently revealed several crush fractures of my vertebrae.

Overall, though, most of the hospital staff were good and very dedicated. My recovery was proceeding at a surprisingly fast rate, and I was doing much better than had been initially expected. By the end of December functional movement had returned to my left arm, and I was also able to stand and take a few steps wearing a prosthesis that had been made for me.

Small Steps
Big Outcomes

When I had the first cast for my prosthesis, I was unable to stand and was held upright with metal clamps around my waist. It was frustrating because I could not do simple tasks that I had done since I was a baby. But, frustration, correctly channelled, can be a powerful force. I knew where I wanted to be and realised that what I wanted could not be achieved immediately and took encouragement from every small improvement I made. At this stage I would reward myself by resting and would sleep for the next twelve hours or so before doing it all again. With extensive efforts and a lot of hard work I gradually inched forward and would celebrate small wins to keep me motivated.

The therapist who was helping me learn to walk again, was excellent. By the end of the first week of January I had progressed from a straight-knee to a bent-knee prosthesis. The timeframe for this amount of progress varies and can take up to twelve months to achieve. I was determined to walk again, one day. In my amputee report my therapist described my rate of improvement as remarkable.

At this same time my speech abilities were reported as being back to normal with no signs of communication impairment. I was also starting to propel myself around the ward in a wheelchair and that was giving me some feeling of independence. All in all I was progressing very well and that was lifting my spirits.

As I said earlier, I received excellent care from the doctors who were looking after me in London but unfortunately they had the habit of underestimating both the degree to which I could recover and the speed at which I could recover. I cannot blame them for that because there are some real limitations that can relate to the degree to which extreme physical injuries can be

Chapter 5
Uncertain Future

assessed. The doctors or therapists can observe the damage, but there is no way that they can tell how well that damage is going to heal. We are all different individuals with varying potentials for healing. Also, my experience tells me that attitude and expectation play a big role in the recovery process and so much of those attitudes are happening inside the head and therefore are difficult to assess.

When it comes to assessing brain damage and the associated healing potential it is far more difficult. The brain is such a complex organ and there is so much that we still do not understand about its inner workings. Clearly a doctor or therapist cannot step into your brain and experience what you are thinking or feeling. They are left to making educated guesses as to what is going on, based on their observations and interpretations of what the patient is doing, not doing, saying, or not saying. My experience as a recovering trauma patient tells me that the experts often fall well short of the mark with their assessments.

An example of this is the way they interpreted the meaning of my various moods. If I had moments when I felt down about being so badly smashed up and about losing a leg, then the experts would write in my medical report that I was showing signs of depression. If at other times I was trying to accept my situation and set some goals for making the most of my future, then the experts would write in my medical report that I was showing signs of having difficulty perceiving the reality of my situation. It seems that whatever behaviour I showed it was somehow interpreted as a sign of some problem existing.

When I look back at the range of emotions I was going through at that time I think that they were reasonable emotions given my circumstances. I had been going along very well through life and was on top of the world with everything going as planned and then, out of the blue, I had it all taken away from me and had to readjust to living as an amputee, with a bunch of accompanying injuries to boot. If I had not shown some emotional ups and downs in those circumstances, then I would not have been a normal human being.

At that point in time I did not realise that I had been diagnosed as having severe brain injuries. As far as I knew I had received some major head injuries, but no-one had told me that I was missing parts of my brain or that other parts of my brain had been severely damaged. I had still been unconscious when I was taken to Queens Square for emergency brain surgery and remained unconscious for about a week after I had been brought back to the original hospital. Also the doctors spent a lot more time talking about me, rather than talking to me. Apparently my family had been told about the extent of my brain injuries, but no-one had informed me. I would not find out that I had parts of my brain missing until after I returned home to Australia.

I might not have known the full extent of my injuries but what I did know was that, regardless of what the injuries were, ultimately, we are all responsible for ourselves and I knew that I had to deal with recovering and rehabilitating in my own way. I realised that my future would be what I made of it. I had a need to be self-sufficient and cope by myself with what life presented.

There were many things, both physical and emotional, I had to address after my accident but the key to moving on is acceptance. It is difficult to work out a strategy to take you to your goals if you do not accept where you are starting from. But accepting what your situation is, is not the same as dwelling on

Chapter 5
Uncertain Future

it. Dwell on what has been taken away and you close yourself off to new avenues.

This attitude of acceptance is particularly important when you have extreme injuries that effects each thought and everything that you do, or do not do, on a day-to-day basis. Those injuries are the starting point for your recovery. Knowing exactly what that starting position is assists you to make the best choices to help you move forward.

However, there is something that is important not to accept and that is any negative or limiting beliefs that others may put on you. With my extensive head injuries and left sided paralysis many believed that the outlook for my future was bleak at best. They were willing to believe that I would need to be dependent on others for the rest of my life, but I was not willing to believe that. I not only believed, but I also knew in my heart, that I would one day walk on two legs again, live independently again and nurse again. I saw myself as a whole and independent person and I was willing to do whatever was required in order to prove that my positive image of my future was a reasonable image to hold.

I had to fight negativity every step of the way. Others would tell me that my goals were unrealistic and that I should abandon them or at least reduce them down to what they thought was realistic. But time has proven that I was the one who was realistic, and they were the ones who were unrealistic. It took longer than I had hoped, and it also turned out to be harder than I hoped, but in the end, I have achieved all those goals and that is the best way to prove that your goals are realistic ones.

When I talk about having achieved all my goals, I certainly do not mean to sound boastful in any way, because that is not the way I see it. I do not think that I have been given any special skill or ability for achieving goals. I firmly believe that many of us can do most things if we apply a good set of strategies and work to keep our attitude strong.

I am not saying that it was easy for me but if you set big, challenging goals then clearly, they will be challenging rather than easy. But isn't that what makes them so worthwhile?

I would also like to make it clear that I was not always positive. I think that having a positive attitude is a good place to be emotionally, but I do not know anyone who is positive all the time. I think that if we can get ourselves to the point where we are positive more than we are negative then we are more likely to be heading for success. During the time I was in hospital in London I experienced many challenging situations, and I went through the full range of emotions, both good and bad.

It can be difficult to remember how you were feeling twenty-five years ago but fortunately I had a habit of keeping a diary and as soon as I was up to it after my accident, I started making entries again. I really appreciate that habit now because reading what I wrote at that time reminds me of exactly what I was feeling.

On the 24th of January, eight weeks after my horrific accident and while still in hospital in London, I started my diary again, and I made the following entries that day: *"I have quite a different life for me now, other than the one that I had planned and hoped for. Regardless of having only one leg, I will be able to tackle a lot more than expected."* And then: *"Last week I had another prosthesis made due to me putting on weight and sustaining muscle build up and it therefore no longer fits snugly...it's great to be able to walk again...especially after just lying there and not being able to do ANYTHING for myself."*

Chapter 5
Uncertain Future

On the 2nd of February, my spirits were a bit low, and I wrote: "*A bit down in the dumps. I really don't have a lot to offer any man at the moment. Why did I have to have an accident? Why do I have to persevere with my injuries for the rest of my life? I am sick and tired of it. I want to be normal again. I suppose no man will want me now ... I'll just have to get use to this type of life. Why me? I don't want this type of existence if you can call it that. I want to lead a normal life again.*" But then on the 13th of February my diary entry was "*Walked back to the ward from physio for the first time. YEH ... I am getting there, I don't care how slow it is, but I'm getting there.*"

I suppose that we are all human and we all have our ups and downs, but I feel if we are positive most of the time then we can push through the doubts and move forward toward our goals. My view is that you do not have to be perfect, you just have to do the best that you can. Acknowledge your bad days and accept them as normal but then move forward and focus on your goals. I believe that holding that attitude is a large part of the formula for success.

On 25th January I had a great day. David had stayed with me in my hospital room overnight then Gavin took me for a walk in a wheelchair along Westminster Bridge and past Big Ben. David had gone to McDonalds and it was while I was on Westminster Bridge that I ate my first piece of solid food in about eight weeks, a chicken nugget! Up until then I was fed via a nasogastric tube and was only allowed to sip horrible, thickened fluids because of how my whole body had been affected by the accident. But I just wanted to eat and taste 'real' food, so I cautiously took a small bite and managed to swallow it. Not exactly standard medical recommendations at that stage but it was glorious! It is hard to believe but that one chicken nugget meant so much to me at the time. It is amazing how something so small can be so significant. It was fantastic to be outside in the fresh air again.

Also, on this same day, while Gavin and David had gone their separate ways to do things, I thought I just might surprise Mum, who was staying in the accommodation quarters connected to the hospital. As was often the case a nurse was nowhere to be found so I could not inform them I was going for a stroll in my wheelchair. So, I just got in the wheelchair and somehow found my way to Mum's room. When I got there, Mum was in total shock and perplexed at how I could possibly find my way to her, in a wheelchair, in the state I was in with my brain injuries and associated PTA, my left-sided weakness and diminished energy level. It also seemed to me that she felt guilty for not being by my side because she was worried that I could have been injured or gotten lost while I was gallivanting around the hospital grounds. I assume that Mum was so worried because the medical staff were telling her and Gavin that I really was not aware of what I was doing at this stage. Mum and Gavin believed the professionals, but I was confident that I knew what I was doing and, since I arrived safe and sound at Mum's room, a place that I had never even been to before, I think I was proved to be right.

Mum then escorted me back to the ward where the nurses were frantically looking for me. They were all in a state of utter panic. I had, before I left the ward, spent time looking for some nurses to tell them where I was going, but as per usual, not one could be found. Anyway, they might have been worried, but I was excited about my little adventure and immensely proud of myself for being able to propel myself around in the state I was in. Mum told me years later that when I got back to my hospital room after my thrilling journey, I was totally exhausted and slept for about twelve hours. On reflection I presume that it would have

Chapter 5
Uncertain Future

taken a lot out of me, and I then needed to conserve my energy again so that my brain and body could continue repairing itself. I might have been exhausted by it all, but I had an exhilarating experience of being outside again and it was good to be out of the ward for a short while.

MAKING THE MOST OF MY SECOND CHANCE AT LIFE

In total I spent around eleven weeks in hospital in London, from the day of my accident, 1st December, until my discharge on the 15th of February.

From the time I was conscious again and aware of my surroundings, right up to the time I was discharged, my most consistent emotion was frustration. I was frustrated by the fact that I was so dependent on others for everything, and that frustration fuelled my intense desire to regain my independence. I was frustrated by having lost my mobility and that frustration pushed me on with learning to walk with a prosthetic leg. I was frustrated by the many ways that others continually resisted my goals and consistently underestimated my ability to regain a productive and successful future and that frustration strengthened my drive and determination to prove them wrong by setting ambitious goals, and then working at them until I had achieved them.

At the end of January I was sent for assessment at the rehabilitation hospital at Homerton. Their assessment was that my rehabilitation was going so well, and I was too good to be placed in their facility and that the best course of action would be for me to return home to Australia to complete my rehabilitation there. So, on the 15th of February, I was discharged from hospital and went back to spend a few days in my London home before I flew back to Australia.

When it was time to leave the hospital, I was thinking of the goal that I had set to walk out of the hospital. I had indeed learned to walk using my new bent-knee prosthesis and so, even though I was being taken out of the hospital in my wheelchair, I wanted to both achieve my goal as set and also to surprise the nurses who had cared for me so well while I was in the ICU. When I reached the entrance to ICU I proudly stood, thanked the nurses, and walked out of the hospital. It felt so good to be able to do that and it brought tears to my eyes. Being able to walk out of the hospital like that was so good for me emotionally. During the previous three months I had been forced to deal with so much loss and despite being frail and weak I exerted myself to improve my recovery status, and that can take its toll. It was an easy temptation at that point in my life to spend too much time thinking about what I had lost but being able to proudly walk out of the hospital like that really made me feel like I was leaving there as a winner!

Prior to the accident I had been living in a huge, shared house with some flatmates and I had been working with a great bunch of people at the Royal Free Hospital. Now that I was back in that house, and scheduled to return to Australia, all those friends came together for a going away party for me which I appreciated so much. Nothing beats having such good friends who genuinely care for you, and are there for you when you need them, and that party reminded me that I had been lucky indeed to have a great group of friends in London who were so supportive and encouraging.

Chapter 5
Uncertain Future

I was scheduled to fly back to Australia on the 20th of February, 1997, after nearly three years of living in Germany and England and travelling to many interesting destinations in a whole range of countries. But I was not ready to go back home to Australia so soon.

My plan had been to see the few places that were left on my list, and then work for another year in London and save money. Then I would be able to go back home with enough money to buy my own house and be set up for life. Before my accident I thought I would be returning home to Australia as a vivacious young woman, yet here I was feeling that I did not have a lot to offer. I was driven to the airport by two paramedics, Ian and Paul, who I knew from working as a registered nurse in the trauma unit and who I socialised with. I had never imagined that I would be leaving England this way and I was in tears as I left Heathrow airport.

When I boarded the plane to fly home to Australia, the Qantas flight steward gave me a bottle of wine and said to me: "You can crack this open after your first run!" That remark from him certainly raised my spirits! It was such a relief that someone was looking on the bright side of things, not feeling sorry for me and not embarrassed to approach me. Lives have swivelled and changed direction on the strength of a chance remark and his positive attitude was just what I needed at that time.

Since my return home to Australia, I have told the story of my accident many times over the years, both to friends and also as an inspirational speaker, and it does not seem to matter how many times I tell the story, I am still affected by just how close I came to dying on the 1st of December 1996. I was so lucky to have survived. It is true that I have had my share of challenges since

Small Steps
Big Outcomes

my accident, but I have also had a lot of great times too, that I would never have otherwise had, and I have done some great things that I would never have otherwise done and met a lot of interesting people that I would never have otherwise met. It has reinforced my belief that even bad experiences, that you would have preferred not to have, can still have their upside if you keep your eyes open for that upside. We cannot always determine events that happen, but we can determine how we choose to respond to those events and that makes all the difference.

Even the biggest challenges that I have had to face have a positive side in that they build character and to me when it all comes down to it your character is your destiny. My experiences have taught me that no matter whether it is life or a horse that throws you, the best thing to do is to get right back on.

I do not see triumph as overcoming tragedy, winning or being the best at something. I view it as believing in yourself and having the courage to continue moving forward in your journey to achieve your goal, regardless of how big or small that quest may be.

When I left London to head back home to Australia, one chapter in my life was closing but another one was opening. I had survived against all odds and now it was time to start my journey to recapturing a normal life. The experts were predicting that a normal life was out of the question for me and that I should accept that the chance of achieving my dreams had ended, but from my point of view there are certainly no endings in my life, only discoveries and new beginnings.

I did not know it at the time but when I arrived back in Australia, I would discover a whole new set of challenges that would require me to dig deep inside myself to discover ways to meet

Chapter 5
Uncertain Future

and beat those challenges so that I could live the life that I wanted to live. I was not really asking for anything over the top, I simply wanted to live what I saw as a normal life. I wanted to be independent again, walk on two legs again, to go back to my nursing career and buy my own home as I had planned and envisaged before my accident. I certainly was not willing to settle for the lesser quality of life that so many others were predicting for me.

Small Steps
Big Outcomes

- We do not know all of the potential directions our life could or possibly should have progressed.

- Chance events can direct the course of your life yet reveal hidden strengths within to deal with circumstances.

- During our lifetime, something that is unexpected or disruptive may occur. Change sparks an emotional response and the sooner you can accept what has occurred the better. I believe that when you accept the situation, regardless of how painful it may be, you can start moving forward.

- Not everything is possible … but views and attitudes can be more important than the mere facts.

- The hidden strengths within us that jump into action when needed.

- We are capable of incredible things when our survival is threatened.

- There is a CAN in every can't.

- Make the best of a situation.

- Acknowledge small wins and take encouragement from them.

- Keep moving forward one step at a time.

- Importance of attitude, visualisation and belief in goals for motivation to achieve.

- Wrestling with negative emotions and pushing them into the positive.

Chapter 5
Uncertain Future

- The role of attitude and expectation in the recovery process.

- The key to moving on is acceptance. Dwell on what has been taken away and you close yourself off to new avenues.

- Achieve goals by applying strategies and working to maintain a positive attitude.

- You do not have to be perfect you just have to do the best that you can.

- Frustration, correctly channelled, can be a powerful force for driving you to achieve your desired goal.

- Determine how to respond to events.

- Triumph viewed as believing in yourself and having the courage to continue moving forward.

- No endings … only discoveries and new beginnings.

- Where there is life … there is hope.

- I see RESILIENCE as not giving up, assembling what is within us to make it through and redirecting what is to become.

Chapter 6

One Step at a Time

I returned home to Australia as a person not only transformed by extraordinary travel experiences but by unimaginable trauma.

When we landed in Sydney, I was escorted off the plane and into a waiting ambulance on the tarmac. There I was greeted by waiting relatives before I was taken home.

It was good to see that I had family members there to support me, but still this was not the homecoming that I had envisioned prior to my accident. I would have preferred returning to Australia as my normal self. Arriving home this way really was quite emotional for me. I did not want this type of existence. I did not deserve this. But, after allowing myself the short luxury of feeling sorry for myself I realised that, if I were to give myself any chance of having a worthwhile life again, I had to step beyond self-pity and pull myself together. I suppose we cannot always control the things that happen to us in life, but we can control our reactions to those events. At the end of the day, we are the deciders of our own destiny. We hold the answers in our thoughts, decisions and actions. If I was going to be normal again it was up to me to make it happen.

I got home via two ambulances which took me all the way to Mum and Dad's place, the family home I had grown up in at Bolwarra Heights. We had to transfer to anothr ambulance at about the halfway mark. I presume that it was more efficient to use an ambulance from each area. Back then it was a long trip that took about three hours, and I appreciated the break for changeover, so it all worked out well. When we arrived home, I had a spectacular entry up our long driveway that had lanterns alight on either side. Our home was surrounded with glowing-coloured lights and *Welcome Home Marny* signs. Inside there were balloons and flowers everywhere. I was overwhelmed at the extent to which my family and friends had gone to, to show that they were pleased and appreciative of my survival, recovery and return to Australia. Their meaningful gestures to try to uplift my spirits deeply touched me. It helped me to appreciate that, even though I was not yet the fit and healthy Marny that I wanted to be, it was still good to be home, especially after some difficult times in hospital.

I got to spend about a week at my parent's home and then it was back to hospital again, this time at Rankin Park Hospital, located at New Lambton Heights which was a 45-minute drive from home. I was in this hospital so that the doctors could assess my condition and then, after another week, I was transferred to a brain injury recovery unit (which I will refer to, from this point on, simply as the brain injury unit).

The brain injury unit was a halfway house for people with brain injuries that were too severe for them to be able to immediately go back into living independently in the normal world. This was the first time that I had been made aware that I had major brain injuries, the first time that I had been told that I also had parts of my brain missing and also the first time that I became fully aware as to just how negative and limiting the expert opinion was as to what my life would be like from this point on.

My time at the brain injury unit was also the start of a long battle between the experts and me regarding my capabilities. On one

Chapter 6
One Step at a Time

hand they were telling me about all the things I could not do and trying to convince me, my family and my friends, that I would need to live a limited and dependent life for the rest of my days. On the other hand, there was me striving hard to prove that I could live a normal life again with full independence, able to resume my nursing career following rehabilitation and to live a high-quality, fulfilling life. I would have many ups and downs during this battle, and I would experience a lot of emotional distress and frustration, and then, finally the joy and exhilaration of triumph.

During this time, I also learned a lot about what is truly important in life, and most of all, I learned that when others are putting limitations on you it is vitally important to realise that no matter what they are saying, you still have the choice to either accept or reject those limitations. The choice you make, and the actions you take, based on that choice, will go a long way toward determining the quality of life that you will live.

The brain injury unit was somewhat like a large house but a lot more clinical and a lot less home-like. I lived there on weekdays and went back to my parents' home on weekends. The therapists who were there during the day included a physiotherapist, a psychologist and an occupational therapist.

While I was in the hospital in London the therapists who were helping me with my recovery were highly qualified, well experienced, world-class professionals. By way of contrast, I felt that the therapists at the brain injury unit were young and inexperienced. As is often the case with the inexperienced they seemed to have very little concept of just how much they do not know about what is required to do a good job. I also felt that they were still at that cocky stage where they thought they knew it all.

Small Steps
Big Outcomes

In reality, they just had not been doing the job long enough to realise that you always have a lot more to learn. In particular, that in order to be a good therapist you need to learn how to listen to your patient and then to adapt your approach to suit the individual needs of that patient.

I was not the only resident in this clinical rehabilitation unit, but I was the only female living there during the week. There were several men living there as well. Apparently, none of them had the severity of physical brain damage that I had, but their functional level was far below mine. They had extreme difficulty doing very simple tasks, such as cooking or bringing in the mail from the mailbox at the front of the property. I would look at them and think: "What am I doing in here with these guys? I'm in the wrong place!"

In recent years there have been a lot of advancements in helping people to recover from brain injuries. But when I was in the brain injury unit, twenty-five years ago, it was a lot more primitive.

The general attitude at that time was that someone with extensive brain injuries, like mine, would never fully recover. The experts I encountered at the brain injury unit had no confidence at all in my brain's ability to repair itself. As a result, they ignored the evidence that was right in front of their eyes and tried to interpret reality in a way that fitted into their model, rather than to change their model to fit reality.

They would look at the other residents and see the functional difficulties they were having and then they would say something to the effect that since my injuries were more severe than those of the other residents, then my functionality must be worse than theirs. When I demonstrated much higher levels of functioning, the experts would just tell my family and friends that I was not

Chapter 6
One Step at a Time

anywhere near as good as I seemed, but that it was just a case of me fooling myself as to what I was thinking and processing.

A concrete example of this was the dispute we had over depth perception.

I was told by a professional at the brain injury unit that I would never be able to drive a car again as it was impossible for me to have depth perception with the extent of my brain injuries. They said that the areas of my brain that were needed to process depth perception were either missing or so severely damaged that depth perception was simply not a possibility for me anymore. I knew I had fully functional depth perception and explained the reasons why I was certain of this. For example, I was an amputee walking around on crutches and had not fallen over and I was involved in dressage, a highly skilled form of riding, cantering around while mounted on a horse on a weekly basis and could navigate my way around the arena without any difficulty. But they told my family and friends I was just fooling myself. I then had to arrange to be tested by an outside professional, one who was not associated with the brain injury unit. Sure enough, those tests proved that my depth perception was perfect.

After going through all this and proving that I did have depth perception, you might think that from then on, those experts would start to listen to me and take my assessments of my own capabilities seriously, but unfortunately, this was not the case. With every claim I made and with every goal I set, I was still met with strong resistance, and I heard the same old thing time and time again: "You can't do this anymore." Or "You'll never be able to do that again, you've just got to face reality."

Small Steps
Big Outcomes

Now please do not get me wrong here. I am not saying that I did not suffer brain damage. I know that I did. What I am saying is that my brain was repairing that damage at an extremely fast rate and as it did, my functionality was returning much faster and to a much greater degree than the experts were expecting or accepting.

When I first arrived back in Australia, I was aware that there was a strange heaviness inside my head whenever I turned my head or eyes and that I was really tired all the time. The experts seemed to think that my tiredness was evidence of permanent brain damage … but I realise now that my tiredness was simply my brain indicating that it needed to take time out to repair itself.

I also initially had some problems with short-term memory and concentration, but they quickly improved and returned to complete normal functioning.

In recent years, scientists have discovered that the brain has an amazing ability for recovering from injury. Different parts of the brain can adapt in order to take over the functions of areas that have been damaged or destroyed. Research has shown that this is particularly strong in the brains of musicians. I have been playing the violin since I was a young child and playing in orchestras both in Australia and overseas since high school. The experts in London believed that learning music from such a young age contributed strongly to my amazing brain recovery. Unfortunately, the experts in the brain injury unit who were associated with me at that time were apparently unaware of these scientific discoveries.

I hated being in the brain injury unit! I was sick and tired of being told what to do all the time. I was a twenty-seven-year-old

Chapter 6
One Step at a Time

woman who had been living out of home for ten years. I was a fully qualified professional and had worked as a registered nurse in Australia, Germany and England. I had successfully travelled on my own through many countries. And then here I was at the brain injury unit being treated like I was a child who was not capable of looking after herself on a simple day to day basis. It was driving me up the wall with frustration.

Fortunately, my dear friends Kim, Paul and Michelle were, at that time, living about a half hour drive from the brain injury unit and they would often visit me. It was so good to see them. They would take me out, away from the unit, and I could be a normal person mixing with normal people again. It was like a breath of fresh air for me.

I cannot overstate the importance of having the support of my friends. I still looked pretty beaten up when I was first at the brain injury unit. Not only was I missing a leg, but my face and head were still looking like I had gone fifteen rounds with a heavyweight boxer and lost. Most people treated me very differently to what I had been treated before my accident, so it was great for my self-esteem to know that my friends were not embarrassed to be seen with me in that condition and that they were happy to treat me the same as they had always treated me. They knew and accepted that I was still Marny, and they were happy to enjoy my company, and I was happy to enjoy theirs.

Kim and Paul not only visited me at the brain injury unit, but also when I was home on the weekends they would come and take me out. Sometimes we would go out to dinner, sometimes we would just go to their place and have a relaxing time or sometimes we would go for a drive. Through mixing regularly with them I was starting to feel that I was living a normal life again, rather than feeling that I was institutionalised. I believe that they played an important role in helping me return to myself and I feel forever blessed to have such wonderful friends in my life.

I was living at the brain injury unit weekdays for almost six months, but while I was there it felt a bit like a life sentence. I had my own room in the back section of the building and that gave me some degree of privacy. A typical day there for me consisted of sleeping eight to twelve hours, as I still needed to give my body repair time, and then perhaps having appointments with the various therapists. I was constantly tested for various functions, particularly speech, but they seemed to already have their minds made up before they gave me the tests and I felt that they did not really see how well I was doing.

One of the things that helped me get through my time at the brain injury unit was the violin. Shortly after I had arrived back in Australia one of my dear violin teachers from school, Cathie, visited me at my parent's home one weekend. She brought some music with her and encouraged me to see how much of my violin playing skill was still intact. To her delight and mine, we discovered that my playing was just as good as ever.

While I was still living at the brain injury unit, I joined the Novocastrian Arts Orchestra, which was the premier orchestra in Newcastle at that time and I attended regular rehearsals with them and played in all their concerts. I had played with this orchestra when it originated in 1991, up until the time that I left Australia for Germany and so it felt good to be back again.

Playing in an orchestra once more was something that I really enjoyed, and it got me out of the brain injury unit and into a much more positive environment for one night each week.

Chapter 6
One Step at a Time

Similar to what had happened in the Fulham Symphony Orchestra in London, an elderly gentleman in the orchestra was kind enough to pick me up on the way to rehearsal and drop me back to where I was living at the brain injury unit on his way home following the rehearsal.

Rehearsing and playing with the orchestra was another important step toward my goal of recapturing my normal life. I was doing something that I really enjoyed and mixing with normal people. Also, as I discussed earlier, playing music is one of the best things a person can do for brain functioning. It has been recently shown that playing music produces more interaction between the hemispheres of the brain than any other activity that has been measured. This means that as well as providing me with great enjoyment it was most likely providing me with the best therapy I could have, and I am confident that it was a tremendous influence in my continued fast improvement and in the fact that my brain function did fully recover from the injuries.

Having to learn new pieces and get them to concert standard also required me to do daily violin practice at the brain injury unit so that also provided me with an enjoyable distraction from the day-to-day frustration of living there.

I tried to use as much of my time as I could doing something that was useful, interesting or, at the least, fun. I spent some time on the computer which was of good practical value, and I also got to have some fun by playing pool in the recreation room. I had always enjoyed playing pool and one of my regular social activities while living in London was playing in a weekly pool competition, so I enjoyed keeping my hand in while at the brain injury unit, it provided some degree of distraction for me and helped the time to pass faster.

As I have said earlier, I believed that the therapists at the brain injury unit were recent graduates with very little real-world experience. I also presented an extra challenge to them because I was an amputee and clearly none of them had received training in how to work with amputees. In particular, the friendly physiotherapist did not have the faintest idea of how to proceed with me. So, I then attended another service outside of the brain injury unit for suitable advice.

Prior to my accident I had always been a keen swimmer and I had already discovered whilst in hospital in London that I could still swim all the strokes, even though I only had one leg. My brain just seemed to automatically adjust for my change in circumstance without me even having to think about it. I then managed to convince the physiotherapist that it would be good therapy for me to do regular training sessions at the local pool. This meant that she would have to drive me there and back, but she seemed happy enough to do that, perhaps she was keen to get out of the unit for a while as well.

Whilst at our family home one weekend, I found out that about a 45-minute drive from home there was a swimming club that held Friday night competitions. I joined the club and competed regularly. This was another chance to be back in the community as a normal person, mixing with other normal people, doing what is considered to be a very normal thing to be involved with in Australia, playing sport.

Even though I was living in a very artificial and clinical environment through the week I was happy that I had managed to start rebuilding a normal life piece by piece by interacting with

Chapter 6
One Step at a Time

my friends and by playing music and sport. However, I was still very determined to be walking on two legs again.

I had arrived back to Australia with the prosthetic leg that they had made for me in London. This was designed specifically to fit my stump, the short part of my leg remaining after amputation. However, because my amputation had occurred only a few months earlier, my stump was still changing shape and size as it continued to heal. The outcome of this was that soon after I arrived at the brain injury unit my prosthetic leg was already starting to fall off and before long it was no longer viable for me to wear it.

I thought it would be a relatively simple task for a local limb maker to make some adjustment to the leg and I would be back in business, but it did not turn out that way. I will be going into more detail about that later in the book but suffice it to say at that stage I was left with the choice of either getting around in a wheelchair or on crutches.

I really disliked having to use a wheelchair so I used crutches wherever I could. If you have never had to spend time in a wheelchair it would be an interesting and enlightening experience for you to go about your normal activities for a few days using one. I think you might be surprised to discover what it is like and, in particular, how differently others treat you.

Losing the use of my London leg was quite a blow to me, emotionally as well as practically. Back in London I had set the goal to be back on two legs again and had achieved it before I left, but now I had lost that success and was no longer on two legs. However, even though it had only been a short time for me to be back on two legs again the experience had proved to me that it was something that was possible to do. Also, having had a taste of being back on two legs reinforced my desire to achieve it again. I simply had to do it! I knew I could do it and I knew I would do it. What I did not realise, at this stage, was just how many setbacks and disappointments I would have to fight through on the way to achieving this goal. I will talk in detail about that journey later but for now, I would like to revisit the first goal I set after my accident and that was to achieve my independence again.

The goal of regaining total independence was crucial and extremely important to me. I had always been a very independent person from as far back as I could remember. It was an important ingredient in what I perceived as me.

Immediately after my accident I spent a period of time being totally dependent on others, even to the point of being on life support. However, I had progressively regained bits and pieces of independence and took great satisfaction with each small step forward. But now, here I was, at the brain injury unit, and it seemed to me that everyone there was determined to put a halt to my progress and push me into a life of continued dependence on others. I was not interested in going down that path so, to help me fight against it, I drew strength from my favourite motto that I read somewhere whilst rehabilitating: *We are the deciders of our own destiny ... we hold the answers in our thoughts, decisions, and actions.*

Most of those around me were trying to make my decisions for me. So much of my day-to-day existence was being controlled by others. They were telling me what to do and even what to think. When so many things around you are outside of your control, I believe you have to grab hold of the things that you can control

Chapter 6
One Step at a Time

and for me that started with my own thoughts, actions and decisions.

Once my mind stretches to a new idea, it never goes back to its original dimensions. I had decided that my thoughts were going to be the key to achieving independence so, I focused on having the best attitude I could, and I tried to think positively about everything.

I believe your thoughts are the mother of your actions. They give birth to what you do and how you do it. Those actions then, in turn, produce your outcomes. I realised that to get the outcomes that I desired I first had to develop the habit of thinking thoughts that were congruent with those desired outcomes.

The experts at the brain injury unit had a professional model that was strongly rooted in negativity and pessimism. That way of thinking led them to believe that I would never be fully independent. I soon realised that sharing my thoughts, goals, and plans with them was only going to result in more resistance and a blast of negativity that I just did not want to hear. I therefore kept most of my thoughts to myself, only sharing them with people like Kim who I knew would be supportive and encouraging.

Despite my decision to focus on the positives, I found that negative thoughts and emotions will sneak in sometimes. However, when that happens, it is often possible to channel that negativity into a positive force. For me, the most common negative emotion was frustration. When I found myself getting frustrated by the restrictions of living at the brain injury unit, and at my parents' place on the weekends, I would channel that frustration into determination to live on my own again. I learned that frustration could be a powerful motivator once it was channelled in a positive way.

Harnessing the power of thought was the first step, then following that up with sensible, goal-directed action. I had some practical issues to address in order to be fully ready to live independently again and I developed the habit of breaking down my goals into small tasks. I then worked on each task according to my own timeline so that I could progressively move forward.

While edging forward towards my goal of getting back onto two legs again, I regularly worked on my fitness, skills, strengths and strategies to ensure that I became so good on crutches that I could do anything I needed or wanted to do. Being continually active on crutches was taking its toll on me physically, aggravating my back injuries and putting intense strain on my right knee, shoulders, and hands. I knew I had to do something to prevent further decline in my physical condition and felt that it was up to me to do something about it. It took me sixteen determined years of resilience, adaptability and determination to achieve my goal of walking on two legs again. I trialled all possible avenues, one being the first person in the world to lengthen an amputated femur bone. In Chapter 10 I will further explain how I needed to lengthen the femur bone in my stump to enable me to walk again. Now, in moving on with my story...

Initially, my short-term memory was poor. However, I already had a well-established habit of using written lists when working as a registered nurse, so to organise myself during this period I simply made lists on a day-to-day basis, and in that way, I was successful in making sure I got everything done that I wanted to do. This became such a habit that, even now that my short-term

Chapter 6
One Step at a Time

memory is excellent, I still organise myself most days with a written list of tasks to do.

Whenever I encountered a difficulty or restriction, I would develop a strategy to allow me to compensate for the difficulty. Those strategies paid off and I reached the point where the brain injury unit experts agreed that I was ready to leave the facility. However, they still did not believe that I could function fully on my own and so they wanted me to move back to my parent's home full time.

I thought that moving from living at the brain injury unit to living with my well-meaning but overprotective mother was a classic case of out of the frying pan and into the fire, so I took matters into my own hands again. I decided that I wanted to live on my own and I started looking for appropriate places to rent.

I determined my budget and made a list of what I needed in a place to live, for example I had to have easy access to public transport. I then started looking for suitable places in the newspaper and before long I had a short-list of potentials to follow up on.

I soon found a place that suited me and signed a rental lease. I was met with great resistance to this idea both from the experts and from my mother. This resistance was not unexpected, I was prepared for it and had a strategy to overcome it. I drew on something that I had learned from my whole set of experiences since my accident, which was that you cannot always get one hundred percent of what you want in a single step, sometimes you have to compromise on your goals and achieve them progressively one step at a time. By doing that you can, over time, create big outcomes and fully achieve your goal. I compromised on my goal of being fully independent of the brain injury unit and agreed that once I moved into my own place I would continue for a time as an outpatient at the brain injury unit. That compromise was agreed to and so I was then free to move out to live on my own and all I had to do to keep the peace was to have a couple of short appointments each week with the therapists at the brain injury unit. I was free again for the first time in the better part of a year and it felt great. It was evidence that my belief in my capabilities was realistic, and I was continuing to move forward just one small step at a time. My hard work, as difficult and frustrating as it was, had paid off.

Chapter 6
One Step at a Time

- I found that by achieving a goal one step at a time I gained greater resilience, confidence and self-esteem. I did the best I possibly could. I did not regret the sacrifices I made to achieve my goals.

- Consistency, willpower and persistence.

- We cannot always control what happens to us in life, but we can control how we react to those events.

- You have the choice of accepting or rejecting limitations.

- Favourite motto: *We are the deciders of our own destiny ... we hold the answers in our thoughts, decisions, and actions.*

- Grab hold of the things that you can control.

- Practice thinking thoughts that reflect the result you want.

- When negative thoughts arise imagine a positive pathway. Channel negative thoughts and emotions into a positive force.

- Frustration can be a powerful motivator.

- Develop a habit of breaking down goals into small tasks.

- Develop a plan of action to take care of difficulties.

- At times when you must progress, moving forward one step at a time can help you to achieve your goal.

- You cannot always achieve your goal in a single step. Sometimes you have to compromise and achieve them gradually, moving forward one small step at a time.

Small Steps
Big Outcomes

Enjoying the view at Bar Beach 2.3.00

Chapter 7

Sport and Music in Recovery

Endings are also beginnings. We just do not know it at the time.

There were many things I had to address after my accident, both physically and emotionally, but the key to moving on is acceptance. Focus on what has been taken away and you close yourself off to new avenues and experiences. I just wanted to continue doing as many of my previous pursuits as possible, including my sporting interests. I also felt that becoming involved with sport, namely tennis, swimming and dressage, all required structured input from both sides of my brain which I believe assisted with my recovery and the formation of new developed areas.

My return to competition sport started whilst I was living at the brain injury unit and on returning home one weekend someone had mentioned a lady who dealt with swimming events. I then contacted this lady and started competing every Friday night at her local swimming club at Cessnock, which Mum drove me to and was about a forty-five-minute drive from home. This then led to me competing at Homebush and the Australian Institute of Sport. I enjoyed swimming as I was in control of what I did in the water, and no one could tell me what to do or how to do things. I then trained more and continued to beat my personal bests.

When swimming, not only was I feeling better physically from the exercise, emotionally I felt as though the water was washing away the toxic negativity around me and I often felt a sense of relief from being in the water. I submerged myself frequently despite the season or weather conditions as I soon discovered that while training and enhancing my fitness levels in the water, the peacefulness was calming and medicinal due to the associated healing aspects while also improving my physical condition.

In relation to my overall physical fitness, I have found that swimming enhanced my general wellbeing, reduced pain in my back and, following the collapse of both of my lungs, it also strengthened my lung capacity. Ultimately it prepared and conditioned my body into returning to the workforce after my traumatic and devastating accident.

I won five gold medals at the NSW State Championships. It was only eleven months after my accident, and I was still involved with the brain injury unit in November 1997

Chapter 7
Sport and Music in Recovery

At the State Dressage Championships 23.11.03

One evening I attended a local meeting with my friend Mark and was thrilled to learn that Riding for the Disabled Association of Australia (RDA) had vacancies available. Having previously owned a horse I enthusiastically jumped at this chance of riding again and became involved with RDA and eventually trained for dressage events.

I enjoyed riding a horse again, as it was an activity that I loved, and it was another sign that highlighted to me that I was gradually regaining normality. Riding a horse improved my core strength dramatically. I regularly trained and did exercises to improve my core strength as this impacted greatly when riding a horse. Now I was riding with only one leg, I immediately became more aware of being connected with the horse and communicating my intentions through body language. Riding with RDA gave me immense pleasure, improved my physical conditioning and was the start of some new friendships.

Small Steps
Big Outcomes

One Sunday afternoon I was with a fellow wheelchair athlete and friend, Thomas, who wanted to introduce me to wheelchair basketball. Even though I had never been interested in this sport previously I went with along him to the venue. While I was at the stadium someone said something about wheelchair tennis. It was from this time onwards that I concentrated on getting involved with the sport and competing in wheelchair tennis.

I believe that we all have an inner source of strength and energy within us when we want something. After being successful in my first wheelchair tennis tournament in a normal wheelchair, not in a chair with cambered wheels that is required for wheelchair tennis, I then approached it with a vigorous exercise regime and went on to become a member of the Australian Women's Wheelchair Tennis Team and in the Elite training Squad. With the support of my coach and members of my local community, I undertook intense training, gym work and match practice and within a short timeframe I was seeded number 1 in Australia. I was delighted as I had achieved my goal and excelled at something I had worked towards. However, emotionally my success was disturbed because some female Australian competitors were negative towards me, and I was informed this was due to the level of my success and them feeling threatened by my accomplishments.

Regardless of the negativity towards me I had much delight in competing in the FESPIC (Far Eastern South Pacific International Competition) Games, also known as the Far East and South Pacific Games for the Disabled in Kuala Lumpur 2006. During 2007, I was Runner Up in the open ladies' singles at the Malaysian Open in Kuala Lumpur and also travelled to the United States to compete in three tournaments where I received a medal for each event: Tahoe Donner International

Chapter 7
Sport and Music in Recovery

Championships in California, Roho/PTR Wheelchair Tennis Championships at Hilton Head Island and the US Open in San Diego. One being a Super Series Event, in order to get tougher match practice and raise my world ranking position.

I competed in the finals at the FESPIC Games in Kuala Lumpur in November 2006

Most of us have to make sacrifices to put our dreams where you want them to be and representing my country at an elite level could never be attained alone. I was taught by my local tennis coach and in-kind sponsor, Ian McGregor, who supported me in many ways and provided me with a fresh outlook on developing my tennis skills. He donated his time and expertise and helped me with many aspects while competing at an elite level in relation to tennis sponsors, grants, travel arrangements and gym supports ... all of whom donated their time and effort. Competing at an elite level involves a lot of hard work, but the rewards are worth the efforts.

Small Steps
Big Outcomes

I enjoyed the social aspect of tennis and competed in local able-bodied tennis tournaments that challenged me and helped to raise my game fitness and maneuvering techniques.

After competing and travelling overseas for months, my back injuries were again aggravated where I had to be hospitalised. This, in conjunction with the negative political interactions from some officials and Australian female competitors, led to me having to withdraw from competitive wheelchair tennis. This was with a sense of dread and feeling that I had let those who had supported me down. I am extremely grateful for their support, but I could not jeopardise my health and threaten the condition of my back and quality of life.

I do not regretfully look back upon the closed door to wheelchair tennis, for then I would miss the doors that have opened for me: Strength of character, for I do not think people realise what is inside them until they need it, it is just a matter of finding it, and having the right attitude to get you through; the people I met; the personal satisfaction in obtaining my goals; and representing Australia at an elite level.

I certainly do not see myself as someone with a disability, but an individual with different Abilities.

I had previously visited the Australian ski fields as an able-bodied person and had much delight tearing down the snow fields. Following my accident I joined two NSW sporting clubs – one which then led to me attending ski camps run throughout the snow fields at Thredbo. At these camps I initially started skiing on one leg. I would use a full-size ski and have two hand-held outriggers which gave me three points of contact on the snow. I

Chapter 7
Sport and Music in Recovery

was known on the mountain as the three tracker, and everyone seemed to know my general whereabouts. I did not want to jeopardise my mobility after lengthening my femur bone in 2011, (as mentioned previously, I will further explain in Chapter 10), so I then crossed over to skiing in a sit ski which is a bucket seat suspended above a ski that allowed me to rip turns using my upper body and outriggers which were attached to my hands.

Whether it be skiing as a three tracker or sit skier I was exhilarated by the experience of once again descending the slopes at Thredbo ski resort situated in the Snowy Mountains of southeastern Australia. I was still able to enjoy skiing as much as I did pre-accident. My holidays and activities were not restricted, and I was still able to do things that I previously did, however they were done with a different approach and planned in such a way to limit setbacks. I felt like the old Marny again, going on a holiday and doing the same activities that I previously enjoyed in my younger years as an able-bodied person.

Physical impairment should not stop anyone from embracing a full life and should not be a barrier to soaring aspirations and striving for remarkable experiences.

Sport was of great value to me as I saw it as a means of returning to normality. I was competing in sports that I had previously competed in, and I was greatly improving my strength and fitness levels. Sport also provided me with a comforting sense of being in control of my own destiny and not as useless as some people believed I was. I was energized and relieved to be getting so much out of life.

Small Steps
Big Outcomes

I believe one must have a good attitude, think positively about everything, always have a go, never give up and be courageous in your pursuits for you will regret the things you did not do more than the ones you did.

The different sports I was involved with urged me into various training outlets that benefited me immensely. Sport boosted my self-esteem and showed that with my structured training efforts I was successful. I was successful in every sport I was involved with and through involvement with the media – local newspapers and radio – I was more noticed. When I achieved elite athlete status, the media were even more interested. Due to comments made after my story was in the paper or following a radio interview, I realised how much I could help others simply by sharing my story.

I had a positive attitude and visualized where I wanted to be. I told myself from the time that I started training that I was going to succeed. When competing in tennis I would say to myself the score in my head, in my favour, to aid my determination to win.

With sport I was action orientated. Swimming I used for fitness and as an exercise to help me lose 26kg. Dressage required core stability and subtle body movements to communicate my intentions with the horse. Tennis involved gym training, coaching and because I was not in a wheelchair 24/7, as are most people involved in the sport, I then did a lot of training associated with becoming more agile in my wheelchair. Then skiing required more core strength and stability. Due to my intense determination to achieve my personal best I made some enquiries and approached a local service where I was then trained by someone who had prior experience with Paralympic

Chapter 7
Sport and Music in Recovery

competitors. His input was greatly appreciated, and my abilities were enhanced drastically.

I have had a lot of fun and have met some interesting people while competing both nationally and internationally and being actively involved with my sporting activities relating to swimming, dressage, tennis, and skiing. I greatly appreciate the support I received from individuals through sport. They are all a colourful part of my life.

My circumstances have made me realise furthermore that I have a dynamic passion for life and an intense desire to get as much as I can from it. I feel that basically it is our decisions, not the conditions of our life that directs our destiny. I believe that your destiny is often shaped by your moments of decision.

Several areas of my brain were ripped out and are gone for good. The right side of my brain was mainly damaged in my accident, which led to my left side being paralysed initially, and now remains slightly weaker. I wanted my brain to enhance its repair and felt that playing my violin was the best form of exercise I could do for my brain recovery as it used many different areas of my brain. My intense and ongoing efforts certainly made a difference, and I have no permanent effects from the damage. Patience and persistence do pay off.

Music had a positive side effect for my recovery where my brain continues to be creative and develop within a variety of musical settings. The damaged right side of my brain controls the notes I am playing with my left hand, and I progressed to improvising with different styles of music.

Small Steps
Big Outcomes

In recent years, scientists have discovered that the brain has an amazing ability for different parts of the brain to take over the functions of areas that have been damaged or destroyed. This is particularly strong in the brains of musicians. I have been playing the violin since I was about nine years old and have played in orchestras both in Australia and overseas. The experts in London believed that learning music from such a young age as well as my lifetime of playing the violin contributed strongly to my amazing brain recovery.

I wanted to play the violin for as long as I remember. I do not know specifically what led me to this decision, but I do remember Mum explaining to me that when she was younger, she would dance around the fire as her father played the violin and that he would sometimes play his violin in front of the mirror. He played in a band at the local town hall dances, and everyone would regularly comment on how well he played. Maybe it was me imagining the joy the musical sound brought to everyone's ears or the result of them dancing and having a great time … but I certainly wanted to play the violin and years later I have continued to play the violin for over four decades.

Knowing how to play the violin, or any musical instrument with confidence, is a fulfilling and enjoyable ability. I feel that violins are surrounded by a romantic aura of mystique and studies have revealed that there are many excellent, lifelong benefits of playing the violin.

I get so much joy and personal satisfaction from playing my violin and feel that playing it builds character in many ways. One character-building aspect is that it encourages me to continually improve. The violin is a sensitive instrument and I have always

Chapter 7
Sport and Music in Recovery

strived to increase my abilities when practicing or rehearsing with others. Ultimately, this influences my life choices.

Playing the violin offers me an emotional outlet and provides me with an opportunity to release my feelings. For this reason, I enjoy playing many styles of music either on my own or with different people. I like playing on my own as it brings out a lot of emotion and I can wholeheartedly put my feelings into playing the music. Playing my violin with others is also pleasant, with a lot of variety and cohesive enjoyment. I have been involved with orchestras, theatre companies, Gilbert and Sullivan, Irish and folk music, flamenco styles, solo performances, various string ensembles, church groups that play for mass and turning up to open mic nights and accompanying others who ask me to join in. My mood is uplifted by the positive responses gained from performing and respectful audiences.

One orchestral group in which I am welcomed with open arms and am honoured to be playing within is called the Barbarians. Each year, thirty-two to thirty-six participants gather for our major annual concert and, as always, we play for charity, fundraising or just for the heck of it. This group of talented musicians is named after the Barbarians Rugby Football Club in London. Whenever a notable national rugby team undertakes a major tour of the British Isles, the Barbarians form a team of invited international players for the final match against that touring team. The Barbarians come together at the last minute, with minimal training time, and then throw caution to the wind during the match, with fast open attacking rugby as their game plan. And so it has been with our particular orchestra. Adventurous programming, challenging music, no over-rehearsing, just go and have fun and give the music a red-hot go. We certainly do not take ourselves too seriously … just relax and enjoy ourselves while playing in the company of an adventurous group of people.

I am grateful towards those who appreciate something I love. Their recognition is genuine where my physical condition does not affect musical recognition.

Playing the violin uplifts my mood and at times it feels as though it resonates my soul. Practicing pieces on my violin gives me great pleasure and I wish I had more time to increase this delightful and rewarding activity. I not only feel that music provided twofold rehabilitation for my brain injuries, but it also supplied me with a way of expressing myself and releasing various emotions. With the multiple positive effects that music has had on my existence, I ask: Could music be the best medicine for life?

Unfortunately, in 2020, orchestra rehearsals were abandoned until further notice due to the COVID-19 pandemic, but I continued to play my violin in two churches - the Sacred Heart Cathedral Newcastle and St Joseph's East Maitland Church. Initially the services were live streamed at Sacred Heart Church with myself on the violin and an organ player, my friend and music teacher from high school Anne Millard, (who is the Director of Music at Sacred Heart Cathedral). And also, at St Joseph's East Maitland Church where I have met some welcoming individuals and formed new friendships.

I have recently been asked to lead the Maitland Musical Society Orchestra for 2023 and look forward to developing new friendships, musical teamwork and playing enjoyable music for audiences / functions locally with a friendly group of musicians.

Chapter 7
Sport and Music in Recovery

There are many psychological benefits that music creates and socially I believe music brings people closer together, heightens our sense of community and strengthens social bonds. I have found that music plays a significant role in our life, profoundly more than just a source of leisure or entertainment.

Small Steps
Big Outcomes

- Can you think of something that ended in your life ... and as a result of this opened doors you would never have considered before?

- Opportunities can slip by if you focus on what has been removed or negative outcomes.

- Is there an inner source of strength and energy within you when you desperately want something?

- Making sacrifices to achieve your dreams.

- It is our decisions, not the conditions of our life, that directs our destiny.

- Positive attitudes and visualisation can lead to success.

Chapter 8

Patience and Determination

I have already mentioned earlier that during my time at the brain injury unit there had been a strong, ongoing conflict between their rehabilitation goals for attempting to prepare me for a life of being dependent on others and my rehabilitation goals for resuming my life of full independence. Bearing in mind this difference in goals I am sure you can see that when I made that first move out of the unit and back into the real world it was a special and uplifting moment for me. Moving out and successfully living on my own was concrete proof that independence was real for me again. It was also concrete proof that my goals were realistic after all and that the uninspiring goals that the experts were trying to set for me were far too conservative. Now that I was proving to myself that I was on the right track with my goal for personal independence that also strengthened my resolve to achieve my other goals.

I moved out of the brain injury unit and into my newly rented apartment in August 1997, just nine months after my horrific accident. It was very satisfying to be living on my own and fully independent for the first time since the accident. The personal freedom was tremendous, and I had a real feeling of triumphing over the odds.

A variety of people had told me many times that I would never be able to live again at a fully independent level. They told me that the best I could hope for was to live with my mother, or some other carer, and be dependent on them for the rest of my life. So many times, I had heard the experts say that I had to accept that my independent life was over. But I never accepted that. I always knew, deep within me, that I would return to independent living and here I was proving that my assessment was right, and I was loving it. It was a lot of hard work, and extremely tiresome, but my improvements and success with strengthening my abilities gave me the confidence to keep moving forward, one small step at a time, and the outcome far exceeded expectations.

Personal development experts often talk about the need to stretch your comfort zone if you want to move forward in life. I believe that being out of your comfort zone and doing things that you are not always comfortable with challenges you and leads to a discovery of your limits. A motto I have come across somewhere is: *life begins where your comfort zone ends*, but what I think is not discussed often enough is how your goal setting can affect the comfort zone of those around you and how to best handle their reactions to having their comfort zone stretched by your goals. Sometimes I felt as though others were threatened by my determination and I would acknowledge this, maintain my courage and persist in moving forward.

Most of us exist as members of various groups. These groups include our family group, our group of friends, our work colleagues and so on. I have come to believe that whenever we are striving to improve ourselves, we can sometimes also threaten the status quo of those various groups that we function within. At times some of the members of those groups may be up to the challenge and are happy to move forward with us, or at least be happy for us to move forward on our own. However, at times some members of the various groups I was part of

Chapter 8
Patience and Determination

appeared to be enjoying a level of emotional security by not challenging themselves too much and were much more resistant to change. I respect that we all deal with things differently and despite the negativity around me I continued to be driven and productive.

Experience has led me to believe that sometimes group members become so dependent on their need to feel emotionally secure at all times that they will do everything they can to maintain the status quo within their group. For those members their sense of security is under threat whenever one of the members start stretching beyond the group norm and that is when you may experience direct resistance to your goals from those around you. Given my resilience, adaptability and determination I have found that I am capable of doing things where the process is uniquely different to the norm, yet I am able to get the results I want and positively contribute to those I am involved with or working with.

I had come across many roadblocks while striving to regain independence but given the extent of my injuries and associated setbacks, that was to be expected. I think most people will run into some walls sooner or later when they are striving for a goal. However, it is not how many walls you come to that is important, the truly important thing that makes all the difference in life is how many times you choose to find a way over, or under, or around, or through a wall, so that you can keep moving forward. I had found a way past my walls at the brain injury unit and now I was achieving my goal of regaining my independence.

I already passed my driving test in July 1997 and had my licence officially reinstated, but I did not yet have a car. I took this into account when looking for a place to live and so I made sure that

Small Steps
Big Outcomes

I had public transport close by to get to the supermarket, go to the swimming pool, to my orchestra commitments, to medical appointments and whatever else I might need to do.

I had taken the ten years of living independently prior to my accident for granted, but now, after losing my independence for nine months and being told that its loss would be permanent, I was revelling in the sense of freedom that independence brings. I really felt that I was taking back control over my life, and I was going to make the most of it this time around, no more taking it for granted for me! One of the impacts my traumatic accident has had on my outlook on life is that when something bad or unacceptable occurs in your life you have three alternatives: let if define you, let it destroy you or let it strengthen you.

It is amazing the simple pleasures you can get from living on your own. I really appreciated being able to go to bed when I wanted to, to get up when I wanted to, to decide for myself what I was going to do that day and a hundred other little things that confirmed that I was a free person again. Being on my own enables me to truly listen to what is deep inside me. My sense of contentment, despite the difficulties I was facing, allowed me to appreciate how far I had come and be grateful for being able to forge ahead slowly but surely.

I still had my challenges to face because I was an amputee in a world that was basically designed for able bodied people, but with a positive attitude and some creative thinking, I found that I could get around virtually any problem. However, it was necessary for me to be disciplined and manage the resources I had efficiently.

When you live your life on crutches you soon discover that it is very different to living day to day on two legs. Some of the things

Chapter 8
Patience and Determination

that had been very simple for me previously had now become real challenges. One simple example is carrying a plate of food. When I was on two legs I could simply pick-up the plate with one hand, then walk to where I want to put it down and then place it wherever I wanted it to be. The problem when I was on crutches was that I needed to use both hands in order to use my crutches so there was no free hand available to pick up a plate of food. So many of the things that most people do as part of their everyday life were now each posing their own particular challenges to me.

One of the easiest housekeeping tasks for me as an able-bodied person was using a vacuum cleaner, but I soon discovered that doing this on three legs (by three legs I mean my one remaining leg plus two crutches), a back injury and other afflictions, this task is very difficult, very tiring and very frustrating. Despite the various frustrations that I have often had since my accident, I also had the positive outcome of learning some valuable lessons from my experiences.

One of the most powerful lessons that I learned during the first year after my accident was, and still is, the importance of gratitude. By expressing gratitude, I was acknowledging and enjoying happiness for that given moment. Many of us tend to take various things in life for granted and often forget to be grateful for what we have. I feel that it is important to sit back now and again and just appreciate all that you have. Personally, I do not dwell on the past or the future, I celebrate how lucky I am to be alive and be happy about being present in the moment. I try to focus on what is going well for me rather than the negative aspects. I believe perspective is your own choice and the easiest way to change that point of view is through gratitude, by identifying and being grateful for the positives.

Small Steps
Big Outcomes

Even when some things go wrong for us and we are tempted to feel sorry for ourselves, if we just take a little time to look around us at those who are less fortunate, we will soon conclude that we have a lot going for us. My accident has had the side effect of bringing into focus for me all that I do have and, by doing that, it has helped me develop the daily habit of feeling gratitude for the amazing opportunities in life.

One of the things that really helped me focus on the positive side of my situation was reaching the one-year mark after my accident. During the first twelve months after my accident, it was easy for me to slip into the pattern of thinking along the lines of: "This time last year I still had both legs and I was nursing, but now I don't have either of those things." Such thoughts made it easy for me to have periods of feeling sad and wondering why this had happened to me. However, when I reached that one-year mark, I could think: "This time last year I was unconscious in hospital and was expected to die, or at best, to have a totally dependent life, but look at the amazing progress I have made since then. I am now living independently and moving forward with my life." There is no doubt in my mind that, generally, what a person thinks determines what their life is like and the direction that they are moving in. Reaching that one-year mark made it so much easier for me to think positive thoughts and to be grateful for what I did have, rather than being depressed about what I had lost.

I found that life is too short to simply sit back and watch it go by. Determination is required to create change. I feel the longer you remain in a situation that is not working for you, the longer you deny yourself the moments to experience true happiness and personal satisfaction.

Chapter 8
Patience and Determination

Having proved to myself that I was right about being able to live independently again I felt that it was time to start planning my strategy for returning to my career as a registered nurse.

In view of my background and how I was feeling both physically and emotionally I realised that in achieving my goal of returning to work as a registered nurse, I needed to take things gradually and it would require structure, determination, and action.

Because of my medical knowledge and insight into exactly what was required to work in my profession, I was very realistic about what it would take to successfully return to that career and be able to work day-to-day in what is often a very challenging profession.

There seems to be something of a trend these days for certain personal development gurus to promote the idea that if you decide on what you want, and then you continually focus your thoughts on that goal, then that will result in you somehow miraculously achieving your goal, without the need for any effort on your part. That sounds so easy, but I do not believe that is the way life works. A successful life is not something to be accomplished from sitting around, wishing that things were better.

It has been my experience that if you really want something then the best way to ensure success is to develop a strategy and then, based on that strategy, take goal directed action every day until your actions have produced the result that you want. Just thinking about your goal and wishing for it will not be enough to produce it, you must put those thoughts into actions if you want things to change for the better. Personally, it was crucial for me to be ambitious, driven and self-motivated. With consistency, willpower and persistence I structured how I was going to return to my nursing profession.

I was still tiring easily and so I knew that getting back to full working capacity would involve a gradual process. I realised that I would need to get my fitness back if I wanted to regularly work eight hours a day again. I had always enjoyed swimming throughout my school years and as an adult prior to my accident, so I decided that this was an ideal way to strengthen my lungs and damaged body. I spent time each day swimming two kilometres at a local pool. I was also competing in swimming each Friday night and so that gave me a way to independently measure whether my training was leading to improvement.

I had started swimming again when I was in the hospital in London where they had a pool for patients to make use of as part of their rehabilitation. The physiotherapist there thought that having only one leg would require me to relearn how to swim and given my condition at that point in time, thought that I would probably sink when I first tried to swim again. However, this was not the case. From the very first time back in the pool I found that I could still successfully do all the strokes and that I somehow automatically adjusted to one leg without even thinking about it. It is amazing what the human brain can do and how well it can adjust to changes in our circumstances.

In addition to preparing myself for the physical demands of my return to full time work, I also knew that if I wanted to gain employment again as a registered nurse then I would also have to prove to others that I was truly capable of functioning in the workforce again, particularly since I was now on crutches, so I started doing regular volunteer work for fifteen hours per week.

Chapter 8
Patience and Determination

This covered a variety of tasks including being a receptionist and tutoring children who had literacy problems. I then progressed to doing volunteer work in a hospital as this was the environment I was ultimately seeking employment within.

My experience at the brain injury unit had shown me that even the experts underestimated what you can do after a brain injury so I was prepared for the possibility that my ability to nurse again might also be underestimated by potential employers. My strategy to counteract this was to enrol in further nursing studies. In this way I could show that I was fully capable of acquiring new knowledge and that I was still fully capable of understanding and performing what was required of me as a registered nurse. I successfully completed a specialist nursing qualification in immunisation, and I also successfully completed my certificate to be a workplace trainer and assessor. This was further proof that I had retained my previous knowledge and could acquire and apply new knowledge.

Working on so many areas of physical fitness, strength, and endurance, plus study and the emotional demands of working to regain a full and productive life was exhausting at the time and I often just needed to relax and recuperate. I could do that better alone and so I found that I preferred to keep my own company much of the time. I still spent some time socialising with friends and placed a high value on the strong friendships that I had, but there was a certain and, I think necessary, peace of mind that came from spending regular time alone.

I wanted results with a positive outcome and was prepared to put in the hard work to achieve what I wanted. Getting myself to the point where I could return to my nursing career was a slow process and it took me around three years to achieve it. During this time, I also had to get used to living my day-to-day life as an amputee on crutches and that meant that some things which had once been easy were now presenting me with a challenge.

I mentioned earlier that an example of doing something that had previously been easy for me to do was vacuuming the house. Prior to my accident, this had been a very simple housekeeping task. But now it was painful, difficult and tiring. This was very frustrating and could easily have led me to feeling down in the dumps about my new life, so I decided that what I needed to do was to change the way I was seeing the task.

Over my many years of competitive sports I had voluntarily done many difficult training sessions to improve my competition results. I started to view the vacuuming as just such a training exercise and this change of mindset really helped me to get through it. It was no longer a frustrating household chore - it was now a part of my fitness regime and I approached it with enthusiasm.

This was a very valuable lesson that I learned, and it made a positive impact. At that point in my life, there were lots of difficulties that I would have preferred not to have. Some of those difficulties were due to things that I could not change, and others were due to things that would take a long time to change. The lesson that I learned from it all was that the most important thing I could do, in order to make my life work the way I wanted it to, was to have a positive and productive mental attitude. There is a saying I once heard that your attitude determines your altitude, and fittingly the altitude I wanted in my life was to be at the top again. I also decided that if I was going to climb back up the ladder of life to where I wanted to be that it would be my attitude that would take me there.

Chapter 8
Patience and Determination

The attitude that had already been helping me since my accident was to focus on potential solutions rather than on problems and also keep my sights set on where my goals would take me rather than to be distracted by the difficulties I was experiencing at that moment. It would have been easy to slip into the attitude that I was a person with a disability, after all, that is what most people were telling me, but I chose not to do that. I chose to see myself as a person with different abilities. I chose to look toward my strengths and how I could use them rather than to feel sorry for myself and the things that I had lost.

Keeping a positive attitude is not always easy, but I found that there was one thing which really helped me and that was the strong feeling that I had survived my life-threatening accident for a reason. I believed that my survival indicated that I still had something important to achieve in life, some way that I could contribute to the world. This belief gave me strength during challenging times, and it still gives me strength today when I face difficulties.

I feel that having a strong belief in a life purpose is not only a valuable attitude that has helped me, but that it is also a valuable attitude for everyone to adopt for themselves. I am hoping that by writing this book about my experiences and, by discussing the various lessons I have learned from living through those experiences, I can help others to discover or to set a life purpose for themselves. I want to help you gain the strength needed to set and achieve inspiring goals that will enhance both your own life and also the lives of those around you.

Over the first six months of reclaiming my independence I called on the strength of my belief many times in order to help me tackle and solve most of the challenges I was presented with.

Small Steps
Big Outcomes

With every difficulty solved I was taking one small step closer to returning to full normality and to the point where I would be ready to re-enter my profession.

Also, as I was getting fitter, I increased my involvement in sports which further helped my fitness and gave me a much-appreciated sense of achievement. I would regularly travel with friends to Sydney to train for sitting volleyball and, over time, I grew closer to one of those friends, Mark, and we became a couple.

Throughout the time I spent travelling around for various sports I was still living in the house that I first moved into after leaving the brain injury unit. The only downside of that one-bedroom unit was, because of my need to be close to public transport, I had chosen a place that was on a busy main road, with the side effect that it was very noisy. Since then, I had managed to buy a car and was not reliant on public transport anymore. So, when my lease expired, I wanted to move into somewhere quieter. Mark and I thought that it would be good to move in together and we found a nice quiet unit to live in that was out of the city and surrounded by nature.

During this time, I still had a lot of challenges to work through in trying to get a prosthetic leg that was not too painful to wear. However, on the positive side my fitness was improving due to my regular swimming. Mark was also a swimmer, and I now had a training partner to swim with - which was great! I was happy that my training was paying off and that I had reached a good level of physical fitness again.

Through all the practice I was getting I had become a real expert at functioning day to day on crutches and had reached a point

Chapter 8
Patience and Determination

where, with some appropriate strategies, I could do virtually anything that an able-bodied person could do.

Also, my studies had gone very well, and I had passed everything with excellent grades. I decided that I had met the standards I had set myself to prove that I was ready to return to nursing again and I began talking to an employment agency.

The employment agency told me that they needed proof that I had recovered to the point where I really was independent again and truly capable of returning to my profession. They quizzed me on every aspect of my day-to-day life. One of their questions was about how I did my grocery shopping. I said that Mark and I usually did the shopping together and they decided that this was proof that I was not really independent after all. They said that there must also be other things that I had forgotten to mention to them, and they were not prepared to help me return to nursing. I felt that it was a ridiculous conclusion and that it was just evidence of the bias that exists against individuals who had acquired major injuries, even though I had clearly recovered and was living normally again. To this day I am still the only person I have ever heard of who was ruled unfit to work because they did their grocery shopping with their fiancé! I was frustrated as this support service for people with a disability was putting limitations on my capacity to function. I was incredibly determined to work again and, because of the negativity towards me, I was forced to redirect my approach to achieve this.

I had been with Mark for two years and was living with him, but because I needed to prove to the employment agency that I could live independently, I moved away from Mark and into a unit on my own again as I desperately wanted to return to my chosen nursing career. It was a difficult decision for me to break off our engagement but with opposing forces, negativity from my mother, who was trying to protect me, and the significance of my strong desire to return to nursing as soon as possible after my accident, it was a decision that was sadly accepted by Mark, who I remain good friends with. A few months after I proved I could live independently, I abandoned the employment agency because of their narrow mindedness and applied for my first paid nursing job since my accident in 1996. When I received a letter to notify me I had an interview, I contacted the service to inform them that I was an amputee who mobilised on crutches. The gentleman on the interview panel said he was aware of that and stated: "We know this because you are famous." I had recently been in the local paper for my success with dressage and horse riding and he had obviously read of some of my recent achievements. Anyway, I got the job and was back in my profession working as a registered nurse again. That was late 1999 and, at the time of writing this book in 2022, I am still working as a registered nurse. So much for the experts who were convinced that I would never be able to work in my profession again.

What I needed and wanted most was to live my life the way I chose how, including my work. In the years since returning to nursing I have worked in virtually all aspects of the profession. I have worked in hospitals, in aged care facilities, in private medical practice and in both the public and private systems. I have worked in a wide variety of fields from trauma through to chronic disease management, and just about everything in between. Those twenty-three years that I have been back in nursing have given me the opportunity to help a large number of people in need and given me great personal and professional satisfaction. There have been practical rewards too, such as

Chapter 8
Patience and Determination

enabling me to buy my own home. I will fight for the things that give meaning to my life!

This causes me to reflect again on the importance of not accepting the negative assessments of others, even if those others are wearing the label of expert. If I had taken on board the negative assessment of others and set my goals according to what they believed to be reasonable aspirations, then I would never have lived independently again. I would not have been working as a registered nurse again for the last twenty-three years and I would not have been able to buy my own home.

I sometimes wonder how many people are living well below their potential simply because they have allowed themselves to be negatively influenced by those who lacked faith in them. At the end of the day, you do not really need the faith of others, what you do need is faith and belief in yourself. It is very important that you do not allow the disbelievers to undermine your faith in yourself. There will always be disbelievers, the world is full of them, but you can choose to stand strongly behind your self-belief and choose to set and achieve your own inspiring goals in your life. I believe in the power of the mind. I want to be a shining example that with mental fortitude the sky is the limit.

Within reason, I feel that the more you are told by others that your goal is not achievable for you the more determined you need to become to prove those people wrong. When I would hear the doubts and discouragement of others, I would tell myself that their negative opinions would not change what I wanted to achieve. Then I would remind myself that the important things that determine my level of success are attitude, motivation, persistence, drive and initiative. I would tell myself that these things are things that I can control because they are part of my own mindset. This habit of self-talk and self-encouragement served me well and I think that it is something that everyone can do. We all talk to ourselves and what we say to ourselves over and over on a regular basis eventually becomes our belief system, for better or for worse. I believe choosing what we say to ourselves carefully is a very important part of life. Before we can create the life we want to lead, we have to believe what we imagine. Great outcomes start with a clear visualisation of the future.

I know that life's challenges have toughened me, but I am sure they have not hardened me. There is an important difference between the two. I was simply igniting a part of me that I had not even known existed and I was using that to produce the concrete proof I needed to stretch my belief of what is possible, even when all the odds seemed against me. If you have not already done it, I would really like to encourage you to dig deep within yourself and find the strengths that you never guessed were there and then use those strengths to set and achieve your own inspiring goals - regardless of whether the odds seem in your favour or not.

Of course, there are some things that are genuinely outside of realistic expectation. For example, a solid, well-built two metre tall, broad-shouldered man is unlikely to become a successful professional horse racing jockey – no matter how much he believes in himself. But possibilities remain and he can still enjoy horse riding. I think the number of things that are truly impossible are much less than most people think and that most people have a lot more potential for success than they realise.

I honestly believe that the various goals that I set myself, over the years, have focused me in a direction that has enhanced my

Chapter 8
Patience and Determination

life and given me physical, mental and emotional rewards that I would not have otherwise experienced. I firmly believe that the same opportunity for life enhancement exists for anyone who has the courage to set inspiring goals and have the determination, patience and persistence to see those goals through to their completion.

From the time of first arriving at the brain injury unit up until I was back in the workforce, I was on a challenging and interesting journey to independence and regaining my rightful place in my profession. At the same time, and for years after that, I was on a second journey, an exploring adventure to be back onto two legs again. In the next chapter, I will talk about that journey and its various ups and downs and the valuable lessons that it taught me. We are capable of weathering hard times and even find opportunity in those hard times.

I was determined to achieve what I was aiming for and persisted in working towards what I wanted. When challenges occurred, I altered my approach to reach what I was aiming for, NOT my decision to achieve them. My sense of purpose, who I am and why I needed to conquer, gave me the strength and energy to continue fighting against what others believed were insurmountable odds.

I have found that by being determined to confront the challenges I was faced with and to overcome them, I not only strengthened my personal development but influenced the outcome by focusing on solutions, having a positive mindset that is not defeated by the unknown and keeping my sights set on where my goals would take me.

Magic happens when we stretch ourselves and work towards something. I believed I was resilient. I knew that adaptability could enhance my situation and I was determined to get the results I wanted. My success with how I progressed when overcoming adversity, despite the odds against me, reveals how small steps can create BIG outcomes. I encourage you to believe in yourself, what you focus on expands. Be imaginative. It is up to you to illustrate the life you want to lead. We all have an enormous amount of hidden power and potential within us, and life is so good when we tap into that and discover just what we can do.

Before going on to talk about my journey to walking on two legs again, I want to mention another troublesome journey in my past … domestic violence. Shortly after buying my first home, I met a man who later became my husband. We lived together before we were married and there were no incidences of domestic violence. Just before we became husband and wife, I rented my home out and within two months of being married I was physically and emotionally abused. He even took my crutches away from me, as well as my mobile, to prevent me from going anywhere or contacting anyone. In hindsight I should have realised some signs earlier. One example was he frequently played golf, and, on most occasions, he would have to replace at least one of his golf clubs that he had smashed during the game out of frustration. Some of his friends thought this was hilarious and believed he needed to get some of his frustrations out because he had raised his son and two stepchildren on his own.

I made various attempts for us to work things out or discover the underlying motives to both his physical and emotional abuse. We went to counselling and during questioning he would reply with comments the counsellor would like to hear. In fact, he described the opposite to his real thoughts and actions – that he unleashed onto me. When I mentioned this to him on our way home after

Chapter 8
Patience and Determination

one of the counselling sessions, he hit me whilst in the car, and I ended up walking a considerable distance home, on my crutches. Our attempts to work this out were futile as he wanted to physically dominate me and not work together as a team. There was ongoing emotional and physical abuse which resulted in much distress for me as well as physical injuries and bruising. I am five foot one, he was over six foot and instructed Taekwondo. I was not physically capable of defending myself successfully against this abusive man.

On the last violent occasion, I was physically abused. I was briefly knocked unconscious, and when I came to, I managed to telephone the police. The police took a long time to respond, but when they got to our home I was trembling, had red markings over me, and bruising was starting to come out. After questioning us both, the male and female police officers said no charges would be laid but they strongly suggested, almost to the point of ordering me, to leave immediately and never return! Finally, I had the opportunity to remove myself from him safely!!! The two police officers then remained in the house to enable me to get some of my belongings and assisted me to pack things into my car. Our time together as a married couple was very short lived, and I then returned to live with my mother.

The toxic negative effects from my abuse affected me physically, psychologically and socially, along with multiple significant consequences in each of these realms. Once again, I had to pick up the pieces slowly but surely and rebuild my life through resilience, adaptability and determination to overcome abusive domination of my frail existence on crutches, one painstaking step at a time.

Small Steps
Big Outcomes

I was more than drained by the experience but, following our divorce, I still managed to be grateful for the positive aspects of my life. I had the courage to walk away and to visualise where I wanted to be in relation to the direction of my life. Despite all the challenges that may arise, along with the associated draining impacts it had on me, I was once again faced with the realisation of how important it was for me to maintain my belief that I could get through this in very small, incremental steps. I imagined how much better my life would be in the future away from this toxic environment and found the strength to stride forward. I have discovered that you can choose to alter your life by being courageous and living according to your heart, a life that we unfold without regret.

Chapter 8
Patience and Determination

- Keep moving forward toward your goal.

- The importance of gratitude.

- Your mindset can be changed by gratitude, by recognising and being grateful for the positives.

- Focus on what is going well rather than the negative aspects.

- A successful life is not something to be accomplished from sitting around wishing that things were different. It requires planning and action.

- Strategy and goal directed actions help to secure success.

- Putting thought into actions can make your life work the way you want it to.

- The impact of routine, structure and thoroughly utilising resources.

- A positive and productive mental attitude.

- Focus on potential solutions rather than the problems.

- Look at your strengths and how to use them.

- Do you believe you have a purpose in life? Would you like to set a life purpose to enhance your life or the lives of others?

- Believe in yourself.

- Factors that determined my success was attitude, motivation, persistence, drive and initiative.

Small Steps
Big Outcomes

- Importance of ambition, drive and self-motivation

- Self-talk and self-encouragement can become your belief system. Choose carefully what you say to yourself.

- Dig deep within yourself and discover your hidden strengths.

- Enrich your life by setting uplifting goals and be determined to accomplish them.

- Have the courage to move forward when negativity surrounds you ... you are capable!

- When challenges occur, I alter my approach to reach what I am aiming for, NOT my decision to achieve them.

- My determination is influenced by - focusing on solutions, being optimistic and striving towards the outcome of my success.

- Possibilities arise when we apply ourselves and work towards what we want.

- Believe in yourself, what you focus on expands.

- Small steps can create BIG outcomes. It is up to you to illustrate the life you want to lead.

- Magic happens when we stretch ourselves and work towards something.

- Determination, patience and persistence create an invincible combination for success.

- Believe in yourself.

Chapter 8
Patience and Determination

- Trust your abilities.

- Our lives reflect our thoughts

- Be imaginative, it's up to you to illustrate the life you want to lead.

- Resilience, Adaptability and Determination – Marny's RAD Conquest Method

Chapter 9

Strength in Adversity

You may remember in an earlier chapter I explained that while I was still in the hospital in London the experts there had made a prosthetic leg for me, and I had proudly walked out of the hospital on that leg. It was good to be back on two legs again, but unfortunately that situation was not to last.

The part of the leg that remains after an amputation is referred to as the stump. In my case my leg had been amputated high up the thigh and so my stump was quite short. Also, because my amputation was due to trauma rather than surgery, it took more time for the stump to settle down. Swelling had to go down and muscles had to rearrange themselves now that they were part of a stump rather than part of a full leg. The practical outcome of this was that my stump changed considerably in size and shape over the first few months after my accident, and soon after returning to Australia my London leg was no longer fitting me properly and was constantly falling off, making it no longer practical to try to wear it.

I assumed that it would be a fairly straightforward job to have that leg adjusted so that it fitted me again, and that I would soon be successfully wearing it and getting on with life. I was referred to the local limb maker, and to my disappointment I discovered that the simple adjustment I had expected was not a possibility.

The design of my London leg no longer fitted my newly shaped stump, and so it was not a matter of adjusting the existing prosthesis, but instead having a whole new prosthesis made with a completely different design. However, when I started wearing this new leg it was causing me extreme pain in my stump. My intuition was telling me that something was wrong, but I was assured that this pain was normal in the case of a recent amputation, especially for above knee amputees. I was told that I just had to accept that such a high amputation would always result in pain, and I needed to learn to put up with it. I persisted in trying to wear the new leg but, rather than getting better, the pain was intensifying, becoming more excruciating and had reached the point where it was unbearable. I was confused as my various attempts to alleviate this pain failed and my spirits were dampened as I was being told by allied health professionals that this was now my new norm. I instinctively knew something was very wrong and decided to ask my GP to give me a referral for a stump x-ray. Sure enough, it revealed that I had three large bone spurs. Bone spurs can form along joints when the body responds to abnormality. The development of spurs can also be the body's attempt to expand the surface area of a joint in order to distribute impact or force upon a joint. This new bone growth can restrict movement and for me, was extremely painful.

One of my bone spurs was jagged and had a sharp point. Another was going out to the side. The third spur was very large, seven inches long and seemed to be defying gravity by growing back up my stump. No wonder I had been in so much pain!

I underwent agonizing surgery to remove the large spurs. That night, after the surgery, I was awakened by intense pain and could feel that the main spur, the seven inch long and most painful spur, was still there. Sure enough, to my disappointment and annoyance, it was confirmed that only two of the spurs had been removed. The surgeon had decided during the operation

Chapter 9
Strength in Adversity

that, since he would need to cut through muscle in order to remove the third and largest spur, he would prefer not to remove it, so he left it as it was. I was furious and annoyed as I made comprehensive efforts to search for a trusted individual to remove the main source of my extreme discomfort and he ignored my basic request.

The whole point of undergoing the operation in the first place was to solve a problem that was preventing me from getting a prosthetic leg that I could wear without intense pain. Leaving the largest spur was altogether contrary to achieving my desired outcome, therefore I required a second operation in order to remove that third spur, and it was three unnecessary and tortuous months before I could get that operation performed. Due to the severity of spur formation within my stump, I then required radiation to my femur bone to lessen the likelihood of the spurs returning.

The removal of the spurs all but eliminated one source of pain, but an unfortunate side effect of those operations was that the bone in my stump was now even shorter than it had been before the operations. This now meant that it was a bigger and more problematic challenge for the limb maker to design and build a leg that I could wear comfortably and enable me to walk again. He built a new leg, but the prosthesis was now digging into a very sensitive region in my groin and causing me considerable pain that was beyond reasonable tolerance. I had demonstrated, since my accident, that I have a very high tolerance to pain, but this level of pain was just too excessive for me to cope with.

The limb maker also suggested that there was another reason he was finding it difficult to make me a functional leg. Prior to my accident I had always been slim, but after the accident I did put on some weight. The local limb makers told me that this extra weight was the reason that they could not make a prosthesis that I could wear without extreme pain. Walking on two legs again was my major objective, and so if I needed to lose weight then that was exactly what I would do. Over a period of nine months, I lost twenty-six kilograms. I had reduced my weight down to only thirty-six kilograms. Later, when I took up playing competition wheelchair tennis, I decided that I needed more strength to increase the power in my serving, forehand and backhand strokes, propel myself around in a wheelchair on the tennis court during matches and also to improve my match fitness, so I went on a training program to build some more muscle. This took me up to forty-six kilograms, which is the weight that I have maintained ever since.

Even though I did what the limb maker requested, by successfully losing the required amount of weight, they still had no success making me a suitable leg. When obstacles arose, I was patient and continued to work through each small step in order to achieve my goal. I then thought that strengthening what muscle remained in my stump might help the situation and I embarked on a program of special exercises with that end in mind – but still no suitable leg could be made.

At this point I decided that I might need to go to Sydney to find a limb maker who had the skill and experience to make me a suitable leg. I did some research and found that there was a limb maker there who was generally considered the best in Australia at that time, so I arranged to get a referral to see him.

This experienced gentleman realised immediately that with such a short stump it was going to be very challenging to make a leg that would be suitable for me, but he was willing to try. For over

Chapter 9
Strength in Adversity

ten years I travelled to Sydney (about a three-hour trip each way) anywhere from once a week to as many as three or occasionally four times a week for fitting or adjustment sessions. Sometimes my actual appointment was quite short, but I still had to drive three hours to get there and another three hours to return home.

Throughout this lengthy and discouraging process, the professional limb maker tried many different avenues and I went along with all his suggestions, but still I was no closer to the solution that I needed. After years of trying and exhausting many possibilities, I started to feel that all I had achieved was to find a bunch of potential solutions that did not work for me and that was heartbreaking to have to admit to myself.

Between the local limb maker and the Sydney limb maker I had spent around twelve difficult and agonising years trying to get back onto two legs, only to fail time and time again. People often ask me how I could experience such a long period of disappointment and continue to strive for my goal. There were times during that period that I felt really down. There were times where I felt frustrated. There were times when I was angry. There were even times when I wished that I had not survived my accident. But one of the things that kept me going was to think about how much better off I was in comparison to many other people who had been involved in a major accident. I had to direct myself away from self-pity and tell myself that I would get there somehow, the best solution was yet to come.

I may have had a lot of disappointments, while trying to find a way to walk on two legs again, but in other areas of recovery I had a lot going for me. Most of which was beyond what many of the experts had predicted or even thought possible. I was back working in my profession as a registered nurse. I had become an absolute expert at living on crutches and, through some creative thinking, I had come up with ways to do almost anything that an able-bodied person could do, and I was successfully living independently again. I was playing my violin in two separate orchestras, and I was enjoying a lot of success in a variety of sports. In so many ways I was living a full and rewarding life. I may not have yet achieved my major goal, but I had achieved a lot and I definitely had a lot going for me, which I was very grateful for. The awareness that I had achieved so much and the gratitude that I felt for being able to do that helped me to persist with my quest of getting back onto two legs again. Life with all its limitations, obstacles and pain, is still a treasure. I think that there is a lot to be gained from stopping every now and then to reflect on what an amazing opportunity we each have simply by being alive, especially if you are lucky enough to live in a developed country in this modern age. I just had to make the most of it as it is up to me to decide how I want to experience life.

I also appreciate my good fortune of living in a free society where I have the opportunity to set and pursue whatever personal goal I wish to set for myself. I certainly know that pursuing meaningful goals is not all smooth sailing, but isn't that part of the challenge of life which helps us develop as human beings? Challenging goals that take a long time to achieve can be taxing emotionally. During those tough emotional times, when I was experiencing so much frustration over not achieving my goal to walk again, I really came to appreciate the importance of keeping myself positive by being aware of each and every little thing that I actually was achieving. I think that it is easy to forget, when we are focused strongly on a goal and experiencing times when that desired success seems to be avoiding us, about the things that

Chapter 9
Strength in Adversity

are working in our favour. Each one of us would probably benefit greatly from developing a habit of regularly reminding ourselves of just what is good in our life and how those good things make living so worthwhile. I feel that gratitude is empowering and before I go to sleep at night, I think of three things that went well for me today.

Another thing that kept me striving for my goal of walking again on two legs – one real, one prosthetic - after such an extensive period of setbacks, was the size of the goal itself. This goal was not just something that I would like to have, for me it was something that I had to have. It was a goal that I believed would totally change my life for the better once I did finally achieve it. I found that when you have a goal that is so important to achieve then it releases an enormous amount of drive within you. Even after all the setbacks, my drive to achieve that goal was as strong as ever. I found that I could channel the feelings of disappointment and frustration that came with each setback and turn them into more drive and determination to keep me moving forward.

Now I do not claim to know you or the particular challenges that you have in your life, but I do think that you and I are not the only two people in the world to have challenges. Each of us has our own particular challenges in life and also our own opportunities to set big, inspiring goals that will move us forward. In my case the challenge was to overcome the odds and to walk on two legs again. This challenge was not something that I could forget about, because, from the time I awoke each morning until the time I went to sleep at night I was reminded of the fact that I relied on crutches and was living in a world that did not always cater for my disabilities. This can be very frustrating at times, but it also had the positive side of keeping me totally aware of the reasons why my goal was so important to achieve. I find that where my focus goes, energy flows and I was not prepared to stop searching until I had done everything I possibly could.

Another thing that helped me to keep striving for my goal was the fact that I had survived my accident beyond the odds. Whenever I would think back to how smashed up I was and how unlikely it was that I would survive, I found that I could draw strength from the fact that I had survived, whilst other people who had experienced a traumatic accident had not been so lucky. I could not help but think that there must be some reason that I did survive. I have always had the feeling that I survived because I still had something important to do in life.

This feeling that there is some purpose to it all is one of the factors that have driven me to writing this memoir. It is not simply to tell my story of miraculously surviving a horrific accident. It is more than that. I have a strong feeling that if I can share with others all the lessons I have learned from meeting the many challenges since the accident, I will in some small way help others who are going through their own challenges. You may connect with something I say and consequently create value and empowerment for yourself to get where you want to be, just one small step at a time.

I feel that by going through the various ups and downs on my journey through these challenging times I have learned about setting goals, developing strategies and staying on course - regardless of the setbacks and obstacles. I am hoping that by sharing those experiences, both good and bad, they will all add up to something of value that could help others who want to set important goals and see them through to success. Or perhaps

Chapter 9
Strength in Adversity

just to make the most of life and gain as much as possible from it.

This belief has also led me to giving talks as a means of sharing both my story and the lessons I learned along the way. I do not say that I have the magical answers for everyone, but I do feel that I have learned some very valuable lessons from my many years of struggle and ultimately my success in achieving my goals. At this point in life, I am very driven to share my experiences and learnings with others not just to help them in their journey but also to help me make some sense of, and find some purpose in, having had to go through those struggles.

Later in the book I will talk more about how all these experiences have combined to shape my purpose in life, but for now let us return to where we were in the story.

After a couple of years with the local limb maker and then a further ten years with the Sydney limb maker I had reached a point where they felt that they had exhausted all possibilities and there was nothing else they could do for me.

During all the years that I had been driving back and forth to Sydney and trying desperately to get back on two legs, I also had a life to live.

Back so many years before all this, when Dad had his incapacitating accident, Mum had made the decision that her children were not going to miss out on anything as a result of Dad's accident - and we certainly did not. I suppose that I had learned, or inherited, that same attitude from Mum and I was determined that I was not going to waste away my life while I was chasing my goal of walking again. I was determined that I was going to live a full and successful life no matter what obstacles were thrown up before me.

Travelling back and forward to Sydney was time consuming but I found that if I organised my time well enough, I could still do most of the other things in life that I wanted to do.

Overall, it took me sixteen years to find a suitable solution to enable me to walk again on two legs. During my lengthy and discouraging sixteen-year journey, I continued to work in my career and managed to save enough money to put a deposit on my own home. I enthusiastically competed in several competition sports. I played my violin in the orchestra and two Irish music groups, and I found enough time to have a personal life as well. I admit that I was busy. But as far I know, we only get one chance at life and it is an amazing opportunity, so it would be a shame to miss it or to ignore it. I believed that the best was yet to come.

I do not want to sound like I am blowing my own trumpet here because that is not my intention at all. I just think that it is an important issue for us each to think about. When life whips the rug out from under you it forces you to think about your options. Perhaps to even think about them more than you may have thought about them if life did not treat you so harshly. In many ways it forces you to seize opportunities and get strongly in touch with what is real in your life.

It is very common to hear people complain that they do not have enough time. As far as I can see we all get exactly twenty-four hours each day, not a second more, and not a second less. Some people achieve a lot with their twenty-four hours, some people achieve very little with theirs and most of us achieve something in between those two extremes.

Chapter 9
Strength in Adversity

I believe that when you make sure that you have a full life it helps you cope with the disappointments that also come along or at the least it helps you to continue moving forward.

When the limb maker told me that they had exhausted all possibilities and that they could do no more for me it was, in many ways, heartbreaking news, but in other ways it opened the door to new possibilities.

My initial reaction to being discharged from the services of the limb maker was frustration as I was fed up with ongoing setbacks. I did not want to live this type of existence and I wished that I had never survived my accident! To disengage from negative thoughts sometimes I would place myself outside in nature. I would think of my problems in relation to the clouds, so I did not become fixated on the negativity of my predicament, and it allowed me to see things from a different perspective. For example, when I had a negative thought, I would place that thought in a cloud, imagine it drifting away and think of a silver lining. I was very optimistic and would search for unseen benefits by redirecting my approach and devising how I could positively move forward. I would define any small positive aspect to my current situation, be confident and believe in my capabilities to get me to where I wanted to be, visualise my desired outcome and determine how I could achieve the result I wanted.

My desire to get back on two legs was as strong as ever and there was no way that I was ready to give up on this goal. I began pursuing other possible solutions, mostly by talking with other amputees and by doing lots of research on the internet. My focus was to find a proven solution that had worked for others who had a high above knee amputation that had left them with a short stump.

Small Steps
Big Outcomes

One of the beauties of the internet is that you are not restricted to your local area or even to just your own country, you have the whole world at your fingertips. That made me feel that there must be a solution out there somewhere, I just had to find it. I was online as much as I could, searching for everything that I could think of that might lead me to a viable solution. Some of the websites that I found had enquiry forms and I always filled in those forms in the hope that this would lead me to someone that could help me achieve my goal.

Eventually I had exhausted all the possibilities I could find online and still I seemed no closer to success. Then, as a result of an enquiry form I had filled out a considerable amount of time previously, I received a telephone call that would change my life.

The telephone call was from a young orthopaedic surgeon named Munjed Al Muderis, who was based in Sydney. I was ecstatic that someone from my own country was contacting me! Munjed was working at the forefront of an area called osseointegration and was doing pioneering work applying this technique to prosthetics. Munjed thought he may be able to help me, and we arranged an appointment for me to visit him in Sydney for an assessment the following week on August 5th, 2011, in Wahroonga, NSW.

Osseointegration is a process where a special implant is surgically inserted along the core of a bone in such a way that the bone and the implant integrate to become one unit. Munjed was working with titanium implants of his own design that, once integrated, could become the point of attachment for a prosthesis. This then avoided the problem that I had been experiencing of the prosthesis digging into me and creating too much pain to be functional.

Chapter 9
Strength in Adversity

This sounded like an interesting possibility to me, but I had come up against so many disappointments over the years that I did not allow myself to get too excited. I drove to Sydney to attend the appointment but my thinking at that time was: "Let's just see what's going to happen here."

Munjed looked at the x-ray of my stump and then told me that my remaining femur bone was too short. He explained that the bone needed to be a minimum of twelve centimetres long in order to support the titanium implant and my bone was only five centimetres or thereabouts. However, he kept looking at my x-ray, without saying anything. I did not talk either. I just sat there, as I had a good feeling about this, and waited to hear what he was going to say next. Finally, he said: "I don't know if this will work, it has never been done anywhere in the world before, but we might be able to lengthen the bone."

My intuition was telling me that Munjed was someone worth believing in and that there was genuine hope for a solution here, so I said: "Well, I'll be no worse off if it doesn't work, so I've got nothing to lose." So then and there I had decided to go ahead with the suggested strategy.

That was the start of a history making journey that would result in a progressive lengthening of the remaining part of my left femur bone and would eventually get me back on two legs again.

The meeting with Munjed provided me with hope which was the fuel that powered my body to withstand what I was prepared to endure.

Small Steps
Big Outcomes

- Be guided by your intuition.

- Be patient when obstacles arise and persist in working to achieve your goal one small step at a time.

- Achieving a goal is not always easy ... but doesn't this help us to evolve?

- Remain positive ... most of the time.

- Remember the things that are working well for us.

- Remind ourselves of what is good in our life.

- Gratitude is empowering.

- Chanel feelings of disappointment and frustration into drive and determination to keep us moving forward.

Chapter 9
Strength in Adversity

- We only get one chance at life, and it is an amazing opportunity.

- When life whips the rug out from under you, it forces you to think about your options and get actively in touch with what is real.

- I feel that having a full life helps you to cope with disappointments and helps you to forge forward.

Chapter 10

Regaining Normality

The solution that Munjed had proposed could basically be seen as consisting of three distinct stages. Each of these stages required a number of steps in order to achieve the desired outcome of that stage.

Firstly, the femur bone in my stump had to be lengthened by several centimetres. When I first met with Munjed my left femur bone was only 5cm long and it needed to at least be 12cm.

Secondly, a special titanium rod had to be surgically inserted up into the centre of my lengthened femur bone and allowed to integrate with the bone.

Thirdly, a suitable prosthetic leg had to be purchased. Most prosthetic legs are worn directly on the stump, but this leg would be connected on the titanium insert that had integrated throughout my lengthened femur bone. By doing this it would avoid the problem of the prosthetic leg digging into me and thus allow me to walk comfortably. Of course, there would be some practice time and training required to get the appropriate technique needed to walk on that leg.

The whole process would require a number of agonising surgeries and the first operation was scheduled for November 29, 2011. This operation involved breaking my femur bone so that it was in two pieces and then attaching two metal rods to the bone so that one rod connected to the bone above the break

Small Steps
Big Outcomes

and the other to the bone below the break. The rods were at right angles to the bone, and they passed directly through the thigh muscle all the way to the outside of my stump. They were then attached to an external framework that held the bone in a stable position during the stretching phase. This framework is called an external fixator.

After the operation was complete, the real work of bone stretching began. A screw would be turned at the end of the external fixator resulting in the bone segments being stretched a small distance apart. Then we had to rely on my body to fill in the newly created gap between the two bone segments with new bone cells. Before that new bone hardened, I turned the screw again, further stretching the bone. In this way, the bone can be progressively stretched to the desired length. Once it reaches that length, the stretching process is stopped, but the external fixator needs to remain in place to keep the new bone stable until it begins to harden into normal bone. The hardening process is called consolidation. In my case, I had to turn the screw every six hours for fifty consecutive days. Each time I did that, the bone was stretched a quarter of a millimetre.

We knew that there would be pain involved in the procedure, but because this procedure of lengthening the bone in an amputated leg had never been done before anywhere in the world, no-one knew exactly what level of intensity that pain would be. When I had made my decision to undergo the procedure, I had not given a lot of thought to pain. I knew I would feel pain, but I was focused on the hope that, finally, I might be able to get a functional leg and be able to walk on two legs again. However, once the stretching process began, I was very quickly in a position to answer the question about how much pain would be involved. The answer – it was at the extreme end of the scale,

Chapter 10
Regaining Normality

and it was constant, twenty-four hours a day, throughout the whole process.

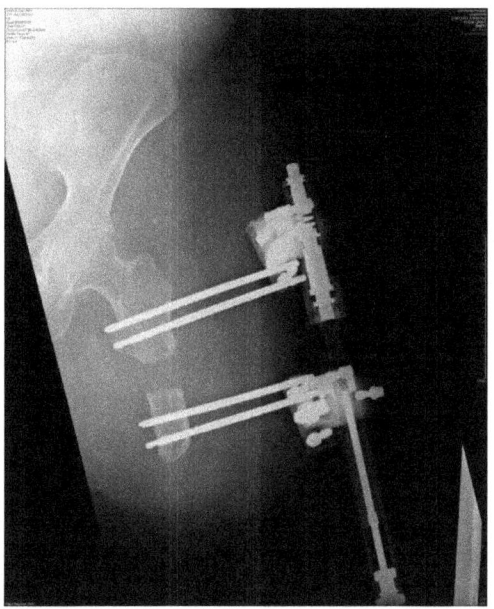

Initial application of External Fixator that successfully lengthened my femur bone

I was sent to a pain specialist to see if he could find a way to help lessen the pain for me. We tried a number of strategies such as very strong tablets and pain relief patches, but it just did not cover the intensity of pain I was experiencing.

As I was determined to successfully lengthen my amputated femur bone by at least 7cm, I set the alarm on my mobile phone to sound every six hours to tell me it was time to turn the screw again. Each time that I had to turn that screw I knew that it meant that the extreme pain was going be extended for more time, but I really, really wanted to walk again. I desperately wanted the whole thing to be over so that the pain would stop but the strength of that goal to walk on two legs again drove me on so, each time that alarm sounded, I turned the screw. I had been trying to achieve my goal for over a decade without success and here was the most promising approach so far. I was not going to let this opportunity slip through my fingers.

The external fixator was sticking out of my stump about a hand's width, and it made it very difficult to do things like getting in and out of the car. I was working the whole time that I had the external fixator because, like most people, I still had to earn money in order to meet the costs of day-to-day living. I was determined to walk again on two legs, so it was necessary for me to adapt to my circumstances and continue to move forward just one small step at a time.

Because it was a totally new procedure no-one really knew for certain if it would produce the results as planned. Every ten days I had to drive to Sydney to check on the progress. The x-rays they took were showing that the stretching was happening and the new bone cells were forming, but they were not showing whether or not that new bone was going to consolidate. The consolidation did not have a chance to happen until after the stretching had stopped. This was a tough time to get through because there was still a chance that I was going through all this for nothing! Regardless, I persisted and adapted accordingly. Eventually, after the stretching phase was completed and we had moved into the consolidation phase, we started to get the evidence needed to indicate that the new bone was hardening as planned and that was an enormous relief for me. It was comforting because my extreme pain and suffering was nearly over, and the desired outcome was achieved. It was now time to focus on the next step towards reaching my goal of walking again on two legs.

Chapter 10
Regaining Normality

After I had been doing the six-hourly stretching for fifty days, the bone had reached the minimum length it needed to be. Munjed wanted me to continue for ten more days to lengthen the bone more, but I just could not do it. Enough was enough! So that was the end of the screw turning and the bone lengthening.

The external fixator had to remain in place while the bone was further consolidating, and so it was finally removed at the end of January 2012, one hundred and twenty-four days after it had been attached. The bone still had to do some further consolidation in order to reach the final degree of strength, but it had consolidated enough at this point so that I no longer needed the external fixator to support it. I was incredibly happy to see the end of that eternal fixator and lengthening my femur bone, and I am very glad that I will never need to go through that again.

I have had some difficult times, often with extreme pain and suffering, but rather than dwelling on my misfortune, I focused on the positive things going well for me and celebrated the small wins and the amount of progress I had made. Most of us have the freedom to choose what we focus on, and I aim my attention on the positive aspects and what is going well for me, remain determined to achieve what I set out to achieve and simply do all that I possibly can to make my dreams a reality.

I followed through on the direction I was given and adapted how I did many things in order for me to persist in staying on track. I simply had to persevere until my goal was reached as my quality of life would be affected greatly if I did not achieve it. I was compelled because the end result was significant in determining how my life would progress. Through concentration and direction of my efforts, clarity was gained, and I prioritised events in my life to enable me to do whatever was necessary to be done.

I played a small part in medical history by becoming the first person in the world to undergo this type of bone stretching. Apparently, I am not only the first person but in fact I am the only person to undergo this method with Munjed's team. I have been told that since they now realise the amount of pain involved, they have devised a different method of acquiring more bone when it is needed.

I did everything I possibly could to make the lengthening of my femur bone a success. Every day I sat out in the sun for eight minutes for some vitamin D, I enthusiastically drank chocolate milkshakes and ate some beautiful cheese, among other things, to improve my bone density and strength. There were still some pleasures throughout this lengthening process, and I had much delight in celebrating these small contributions to the outcome I was striving towards.

I believe that if you can be resilient, if you can adapt, your body can do miraculous things. Tomorrow is another day.

I had successfully completed the first part of the proposed solution - the bone lengthening stage - and now my bone was long enough to allow me to move on to the next stage of the process, osseointegration. For the first time in about fourteen long years of striving for my goal of walking again I finally had some hard and fast evidence that my goal might soon be a reality. The problem of my stump being too short was now behind me. There were still more medical procedures to go, but I was starting to see a light at the end of the tunnel. In my heart I knew I was going to walk again one day soon. I just had to remain patient, persist in working towards my goal and visualise

Chapter 10
Regaining Normality

my improved quality of life. Thankfully, this was another occasion where my determination resulted in a successful journey.

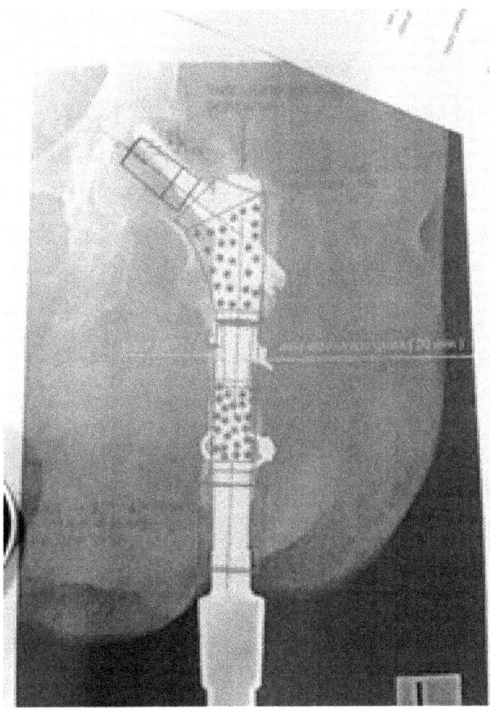

First Osseointegration procedure with implant insitu

The next stage of the process was to have the titanium rod implanted up into my newly grown bone and then to allow it time to integrate with that bone so it would become a permanent part of me. This would require several more surgeries and, of course, an appropriate amount of healing time between those surgeries. You will be amazed at what is possible when you are determined to move forward and excel in life.

Due to my circumstances this stage of the process required seven separate operations and I spent around nine months in hospital.

Small Steps
Big Outcomes

The hospital room I was given for this period was quite a bit larger than a standard room and it had a bed, a lounge, and even a kitchenette. I also had my laptop computer with me, so all in all, I had some degree of normalcy during my long nine months stay.

Because I had spent so many years on my right leg only, my left hip had not had to take on the weight bearing that it would have if I were on two legs. The body is very efficient when it comes to working out how strong it needs to be to maintain bones for them to be able to support the weight that they are required to bear. The downside of this efficiency is that, if that weight bearing is substantially reduced for a long period of time, then the body decides that it does not need to keep those particular bones at that strength level anymore. This is exactly what had happened to me. As a result of this, when I needed to weight bear again my left hip was no longer up to the job and developed several stress fractures. I then required a hip replacement, which meant having four different surgical procedures (stage one and two for osseointegration again, bone grafts and hip replacement) all done at the same time. I again made history as I was another world first where all these surgeries were attended during the same time in one operation.

Eventually I got through all the operations and my recovery was a success and so I was ready to move on to the final stage of getting a new leg and walking again. However, as with most of the events since my accident, there was an unexpected twist to the tale that threw up another challenge to overcome before I could fully achieve my walking goal.

The benefit of undergoing osseointegration is that it solves the problem of getting a leg to fit properly so that it stays on and it

Chapter 10
Regaining Normality

does not dig into the torso. You may remember that these were the two biggest problems that I had been trying unsuccessfully to solve for many years.

The standard approach to making a prosthetic leg is that it fits on the stump. If the stump changes shape, as mine did after getting my London leg, then the fit is no longer good enough for the leg to stay on. Also, because my stump was so short after it settled down to that shape, the limb makers could not build a leg that did not dig very painfully into my torso. By integrating the titanium rod into my femur bone, it had become an extension to that bone, and it was possible then to fit a leg by connecting it directly to that titanium extension and then, with the simple turn of an Allen key it can be locked in place so that it would not fall off. When I want to take the leg off it is a simple matter of using the Allen key again to unlock the fitting and then the leg can be removed. It only takes about ten seconds to lock the leg into place and while it is on it stays on without a problem.

What I discovered after I got my new leg was that even though my stump had been lengthened via the bone stretching it was still short enough to cause a new problem. Because my amputation is so high, it created a lot of leverage on the new leg and that resulted in making the leg quite unstable at times, thus increasing the risk of me falling. And I did fall often!

In one of the falls in my own home, I hit my head on the way down and knocked myself unconscious. When I came to again, I was lying on the floor in a pool of blood with my head split open and I had to then drive myself to my GP and have the wound stitched up.

Small Steps
Big Outcomes

In the backyard with the unsuitable ILP (Integral Leg Prosthesis)

In a follow-up appointment with Munjed, he pointed out that if I kept falling, I could break my hip and do damage that would result in me no longer being able to use an integral leg prosthesis. The only solution was to get a type of leg called a C-Leg. This is a very sophisticated prosthesis that has its own computer chip built in. The program in the chip helps the leg perform more like a biological leg, and it has built in safety features that minimise the risk of falling. The only downside was that it cost around $60,000 dollars, and that was well above what I could afford.

My dear friend Kim has always been a great support for me. Even though we live more than a thousand kilometres apart, we talk on the phone often. She has always been someone that I could talk things over with throughout my whole journey since the accident. When Kim found out about the C-Leg and what it cost she was keen to find some way to help me. She approached magazines and TV shows to see if she could find someone who would be interested in telling my story and helping me raise money toward the C-Leg.

Chapter 10
Regaining Normality

My story was published in *New Idea* magazine, and Chris Bath of the Channel Seven TV program *Sunday Night* also did a story about me and my situation. Between these two sources, the Rotary, and the government body National Disability Insurance Agency, we raised enough money for me to get my C-Leg and an aquatic leg. The aquatic leg is a simple prosthesis that is not suitable for general walking but, unlike the C-Leg, it is able to get wet without causing it damage. That means it can be used at the beach or in a swimming pool.

The help I received in raising money for my C-Leg and aquatic leg has been inspiring and I appreciate this support immensely. When I look back at my whole journey through life, I can see that I have had so many wonderful people helping me along the way. When times are tough and things just are not going your way, it is easy to feel sometimes that you are all alone in the world, but none of us are alone. Every day of our lives other people are contributing in so many ways to the life we are having. Some of these people are people that we do not even know. There are people who worked to manufacture the various products that we use. Someone had to make the car you drive. Someone has to work in the supermarket where you shop, and, if you stop and think about it for a while, you soon realise that so many of the things we take for granted just would not be possible if other people were not playing their particular role in the process.

In addition to those people just mentioned, there are all the people that you do know, such as your friends and family. With most people they play a special role in your life, or in helping make your life more enjoyable in one way or another. Sometimes these people will play an active role that directly contributes to your life or wellbeing. Sometimes their role is more just being there so that you know you have someone behind you, someone who is on your side.

I am grateful for the ongoing support from various people and organisations within my local community, particularly Ann and Judy, who initiated the process and with the support of many others, rallied the community together at the time of my accident. Their extensive combined efforts made a significant impact on my return home to Australia and my subsequent recovery. Various groups like Probus, Rotary, Stroke and Disability Information (SADI) Hunter and Amputees NSW have also assisted me to deal with challenging scenarios in different aspects of my life.

There are many other individuals and groups that have supported me within different aspects of my life and their beneficial assistance has contributed to my success. My appreciation is ongoing and revealed through my diligence in achieving what their support was required for and what I set out to achieve.

I often think about how lucky I am to have great friends in my life. There is a special connection whenever I meet with ex-students or Sisters from St Joseph's College Lochinvar, and the close friendships I formed during my first year of high school have remained good friends all through my life. In particular: Marian, Michelle, Patricia and Jane, who believed in me when everyone else was telling me that my goals were totally unrealistic. They have stood by me through the years and encouraged me and, most valuable of all, they accepted me for exactly who I was, and they still accept me for who I am today. I always look forward to meeting up with my dear friends from high school and even just a phone call can be uplifting for days.

Chapter 10
Regaining Normality

There is also my dear friend Janice who I did not meet until I went to university and had a special connection with instantly! Janice brightens any room she walks into, has supported me immensely and been a wonderful friend throughout the years. We have shared some great times and memories together and whenever we meet my day is always enriched by our discussions and her genuine presence. I trust Janice implicitly for she genuinely has my best interests at heart. It is great to be able to meet up with Janice however brief, just to say hello. And of course, there is Kim. I met Kim shortly before my accident and we also have a special bond that has continued to develop through the years. Kim has always been there to support and encourage me and just to be a great friend. Then, of course, the way she leapt in of her own accord and helped raise the money for my C-Leg that has changed my life. I am so lucky to be surrounded by friends who give meaning to and colour my life immensely. They all have an imprint in my heart.

The goal to walk on two legs again was one of the first goals I set after my accident. It had been a long and disheartening journey with many ups and downs and setbacks along the way, but sixteen years after I set that goal, it finally became a reality for me. I was overjoyed and relieved to say the least. Walking on two legs again has added so much more to the quality of my day-to-day living. Before my accident I took my two legs for granted and never really gave them much thought but after being without one for so long I now really appreciate just how amazing having two legs is and the difference it makes to your quality of life.

Often rewards are gained from challenges. I am determined to make the most of my life and am grateful that I can still live

Small Steps
Big Outcomes

independently and have a second chance at life and get as much from it as I possibly can. I feel that it would have been difficult to progress and eventually achieve my goals if I chose to be a victim of circumstances. I believe that I have survived my accident as I have not yet fulfilled my purpose in life - there is still something more ahead of me.

I have put my will, efforts, and energies towards the outcomes I wanted. I am grateful and appreciative of the valuable rewards that have resulted from my efforts. I enjoy the incredible results that significantly impact on my life and make the most of outcomes and what life has to offer.

Don't wait for the light at the end of the tunnel ... stride along the path and light the way. Forge your own path.

Chapter 10
Regaining Normality

Celebrating success with the C-Leg!

Small Steps
Big Outcomes

- Resilience, Adaptability and Determination.

- I lost a leg but found my feet.

- Finally achieved my goal after sixteen intense years.

- My belief in obtaining my goals successfully motivated me and I simply did everything I possibly could have to achieve it.

- I focused on the positive things going well for me.

- You will be amazed at what is possible when you are determined to move forward and excel in life.

- Patience, determination and visualisation - I just had to remain patient, continue working towards my goal and visualise the result I wanted. I believe my mind-set impacted greatly on the outcome.

- Most of us are not alone and on reflection there are many remarkable people who will be genuinely supportive.

Chapter 11

Motivation and Persistence

Between 1996 and 2012, I had many different experiences, some good and some not so good. I re-established my career, I had great success at sport, I played a lot of music and experienced many other great things as well, but always, underneath all of that, my life revolved around my goal of getting back onto two legs again. That goal was a major factor in determining what I did and when I did it. I had to find the time to travel to and from Sydney to the experienced limb maker there. I had to keep telling myself that I would one day achieve that goal. I had to deal emotionally with the numerous disappointments when, time and time again, a hoped-for solution fell short of the mark. I had to deal with the intense pain that accompanied many of the medical procedures I endured, and I had to keep reinforcing my belief that the pain was going to be worth it in the long run. Then finally, at the end of those sixteen years of struggle my goal became a reality and my life changed dramatically for the better! With motivation and persistence, I achieved an incredible feat. I was motivated because of the positive impact on my life but I had to be consistent in my approach and persist in moving forward just one small step at a time.

There have been two points of massive change in my life.

The first was my unfortunate encounter with the train. My train accident changed my life because of all the things it took away and all the challenges that it left me with. That first point of change is one that I would rather have done without, but I believe that most things in life, even the ones we do not want, have a positive side and my accident was no exception to that rule. The real positive that I gained from that event and its aftermath is that I no longer take for granted the good things in my life. I know from experience now that good things can be snatched away suddenly and unexpectedly and so it is important to fully appreciate what you have while you have it.

The second point of major change was getting my C-Leg. My C-Leg changed my life because of what it gave back to me and the numerous opportunities it opened for me. Now that I have been given a second chance on two legs again, I fully appreciate that opportunity every day and I also have learned to appreciate all the other good things in my life, including the wonderful people that I have been blessed to have known and meet.

Normality is a concept that is particularly important in most societies. Most of us are quick to judge ourselves and quick to judge others to decide whether or not they measure up as normal. For those sixteen years when I was mobilising on crutches, or sometimes in a wheelchair, I was treated very differently to how I am treated now that I am walking around on two legs again.

When people saw me as a one-legged woman on crutches, they tended to assume that I was less capable than I was. Sometimes this would be expressed as a lack of confidence in me, and it made it more difficult for me to get work. At other times people would feel that I needed help and in trying to help me they were far more likely to interfere with how I was moving and, in some cases, threw me off balance.

Chapter 11
Motivation and Persistence

When I was in a wheelchair people tended to talk down to me as if I were a child or someone who was not mentally capable of understanding anything. I don't know if it is true or not, but I heard a theory that suggests that because a person in a wheelchair has the same head height as a child then people subconsciously treat them more like a child than like an adult. Regardless of whether that theory explains the behaviour or not, what is a fact is that people do treat you differently when you are in a wheelchair and often not in a positive way. I don't think that people mean to treat you poorly and I am sure that many people would not even realise that they are doing it, but it seems to be something of a reflex reaction that clicks in when some are talking with a person in a wheelchair. Despite all good intentions, I believe this is a simple barrier within society that needs to be acknowledged.

When I am walking around on my C-Leg I tend to be treated just like anybody else. Often people seem totally unaware that I have a prosthetic leg and even when they do notice, they quickly forget about it and I am just Marny again. After sixteen years of being seen as someone with a disability, together with all the preconceived beliefs that go with that assessment, it is so good now to just be treated as a normal person again and allowed the privilege of being myself.

Even more important than the way others see me is the way I see myself. Sometimes I am my own toughest critic, and it is so good now to feel like a whole person again. That feeling flows over into everything that I do. I feel like myself again and it feels fantastic!

As well as the social difference of being back on two legs again there are also many practical differences in day-to-day life. Everything is easier on two legs than it is on one leg. If you are an

Small Steps
Big Outcomes

able-bodied person, you have probably never thought about what it would be like to have to function day to day on one leg, year after year. Crutches are a great help, particularly the Canadian style crutches, also referred to as Forearm Crutches or Elbow Crutches, that are shorter than standard walking crutches, with a cuff that goes around the forearm, elbow or wrist for extra support and stability. They allow you to balance when you are standing still and they allow you to move around freely, but they do that at the cost of not having your hands free. It might be interesting for you to try a little exercise tomorrow. All I am asking you to do, if you are able, is to be aware, for twenty-four hours, of how much you make use of the fact that you have two legs not one and how often you make use of the fact that you have two free hands when you are moving around. I strongly suggest that you really do that little exercise. It is easy to do mentally as you go about your normal day and no-one else even knows you are doing it. Doing that exercise will really bring home to you just how great it is to have the use of both of your legs and the benefits of having both hands free - these are things truly worth appreciating.

Now that I am on two legs again it is so much easier to do tasks such as preparing a meal, hang washing on the clothesline or watering the garden. When I go the supermarket, I can walk around pushing the shopping trolley because my hands are free to do that. It is so much easier to get on and off escalators and when I am out in the rain, I can hold up an umbrella, try doing that when you are walking on two crutches. There is much less strain on my body now that I am walking on two legs again and this allows me to enjoy just the simple things in life.

There is also one simple thing that gave me great pleasure. During my sixteen-year journey I always played my violin in at

Chapter 11
Motivation and Persistence

least one classical orchestra. The other violinists would walk out on stage carrying their violins, but, because I was on crutches, I could not carry my violin on stage with me. The person who would be sitting next to me would carry my violin and bow, and then they would hand them to me when we were both on stage and I had placed my crutches underneath my chair and safely out of the way. The first time I walked out on stage with my new leg, carrying my own violin and bow was a great satisfaction to me. It is only a small thing and not of great importance in itself, but what it symbolises about how my life has changed for the better cannot easily be expressed in words.

It has certainly been emotionally rewarding for me to see how my long-term friends are happy to see me back on two legs. They are the people who have stood by me through the good times and throughout the difficult years and I feel so blessed to have them in my life. Words can never express what their friendship has meant to me and how much it has helped me when I was feeling weighed down by my troubles. I have heard it said that true friends are hard to find but I know that I have certainly found the best friends. They are there through thick and thin and genuinely care for me and I appreciate that so much. I don't want to lose touch with the friendships I value, and I continue to reward myself with the gift of their company whenever suitable.

Even though I have such great friends I am also fully aware that I have always had a great need to do things by myself. I have a real need to spend some time in solitude, and over the years I have learned that solitude can also be a good friend at times. I think that it is an important piece in the puzzle of how to have a happy life. I had this need for solitude before my accident, I had it during my challenges after my accident, and I still have it now that I am back on two legs. I think that the important thing is for each of us to find the right balance between time spent in solitude and in time spent sharing with others, and then have the courage to insist that you get the balance that best suits you. I value my friendships, but I also need time on my own to process things thoroughly and find clarity within myself.

An important practical difference from being back on two legs again springs from the fact that the human body develops structurally in the way it does because the physical stresses that result from standing and from moving about are distributed through both legs and therefore shared by both sides of the body. When I was on one leg all the time those stresses were distributed through my body in an unnatural and unbalanced way that led to increased wear and tear, particularly in the joints and in my back. Also, when I was using crutches everyday my shoulders and hands had to cope with stress loads that shoulders and hands should not be asked to cope with. This often resulted in pain and certainly increased the wear on those areas. Now that I am back on two legs the physical stress loads are far more natural and balanced and the immediate result is that I experience a lot less pain. The long-term prospect is that I will fare much better, wear and tear wise, as I age - and that is absolutely good news.

As well as those benefits there are also other long-term benefits. You may recall that during my accident I broke my spine in five places. An ongoing result from those breaks is that there is a high likelihood of my back deteriorating over time resulting in me needing to be permanently in a wheelchair. Being so active on crutches was putting a lot of extra stress on my back, but now I am walking on two legs again it is highly likely that I have extended the number of years that my back will be able to do its job. I may still end up in a wheelchair one day, but it should be

Chapter 11
Motivation and Persistence

many years later than it would have been if I remained on crutches. Regardless, I will persist in taking actions that will prevent this from happening.

Another physical difference is the amount of energy required to move about. Living on crutches requires more physical effort than is required to walk about on two legs. So now I feel like I have more energy and everything that I do feels easier. The physical demand of day-to-day living is much less now than it was, but so too is the draining mental demand. When you have to do things on crutches and, as a result don't have your hands free, you have to think things through a lot more and mentally structure how you are going to go about virtually every task, but now I don't need to do that because most of the time I can just do the things I want to do without the need to give them a second thought. I do have my hands free now while I am walking and so I can go about life like most people and I don't have to plan and structure every little thing I do so intently.

In addition to all the physical benefits and lifestyle benefits of being back on two legs again there is another major change in my life that results from achieving my goal. While I was chasing my goal of walking again, I was putting a lot of time and a lot of mental energy and focus into pursuing that goal. Once I had achieved my goal, I no longer needed to structure my time and my life was freed up substantially giving me more time to pursue other endeavours. I had always made sure that my life was not limited by the fact that I was an amputee, and I was already involved in many different things, but now that I didn't need to drive back and forward to Sydney every week to visit the limb maker or spend hours and hours searching the internet for walking solutions, I had more time for other things I would like to do. This means that everything is so much easier to fit into my day-to-day life and both physically and mentally I have energy to spare and that extra energy helps me make good use of that extra time I now have.

When I look back over what I have been forced to deal with since my horrendous accident there are moments that overwhelm me. However, the life I imagined when setting my goals has become a reality. This came about through motivation, patience and persistence. Life is certainly worth living and I will continue to be resilient, adapt to my circumstances and be determined to get the results I want.

My life was almost ripped out of me by the train, and it was then up to me to make the most of my survival and assemble my thoughts and actions piece by piece. At times I felt like I had been mutilated but in the state I was in, especially in the initial stages, I still had the courage and internal strength to go after what I wanted and realised that this was not going to happen straight away.

I was often surrounded with negativity and unspoken thoughts that doubted me and my capabilities. I knew that it was not possible for me to achieve what I was aiming for instantly and focused on my immediate needs and small gains. It was vital for me to remain patient and despite influential setbacks, it was necessary for me to persist in working towards the outcomes I had my sights set on, as the end result would significantly have an impact in my life. It is like I have been given a second chance to live my life and my journey has been very colourful. I am grateful of and very appreciative of the supports I have had but ultimately it is up to me to forge forward along the road ahead.

I positively adapted to situations I was confronted with and became successful in achieving my three main goals: regaining

Chapter 11
Motivation and Persistence

my independence, returning to work as a registered nurse and walking again on two legs. With supports around me I created my own achievements through many things including hard work, determination and persistence.

My priority after getting back on two legs was to spend more time working and earning money. Sixteen years of pursuing my goal had been expensive financially and expensive in time. I not only had the normal costs of living to meet, including paying a mortgage, I also had substantial costs related to my attempts at getting a functional prosthetic leg. Also, I was required to spend a lot of time traveling to and from Sydney to the limb maker and having time spent in hospital for various reasons meant that I was not able to work the full hours I needed to in order to earn the amount I should have been acquiring to adequately meet all my expenses. This had put me under a lot of financial pressure over the years, so, once I was back on two legs, I started devoting more time to the day-to-day task of earning a living.

However, for a goal-oriented personality, the challenge of meeting day to day needs is not inspiring enough on its own. I no longer had that all-consuming goal of chasing a functional leg and I was glad of that because it was a relief having finally achieved my goal, but I needed to replace it with something equally strong that would give me the inspiration and motivation to keep growing as a person.

Originally, when I survived my train accident against all odds, I felt that there must be a reason I was still alive. I felt that I had some purpose in life to fulfil, something I should be doing to make a difference in the world. Also, when I had so many setbacks and so much pain on my way to getting back onto two legs, I would console myself by thinking that there must be some good reason I had to go through so much hardship.

Now that I needed a new purpose, I thought about all those things again and I concluded that my purpose should be to help others. I already feel that I have helped a lot of people through my work as a nurse, but I really feel that, because of my unique experiences, I can do more to help people in other ways as well.

I have decided that I should share my story and share what I have learned from going through all the challenges on that journey and that hopefully by sharing these things with others I can inspire them to find the motivation, determination, and persistence to take control of the direction in which their life unfolds.

I have given a number of talks over the years, and I am now working to increase my focus on inspirational speaking so that I can give something of value to others. Part of that goal was also to write this book that you are now reading. I am basically an ordinary woman who was forced to dig deep inside to find something that would help me grow as a person, so that I could do things that I had never imagined I would have the strength to do. I think we all have that greater force inside us and that we each have a real potential for enormous personal growth. I am now determined to perfect my skills at communicating what I have learned so that I can better help others with their own personal journeys. To help them find and release that inner strength without them needing to experience major trauma to discover their true abilities.

Having survived my accident, I intuitively make an effort to ensure I get the most out of life while maintaining balance. I have come to the conclusion that my accident and the diverse set of

Chapter 11
Motivation and Persistence

experiences I have been dealt with in relation to trauma and associated outcomes, has helped to illustrate the person I have become today and my desire to help others.

In the next chapter I will discuss some of the valuable things I have learned throughout my life, and I hope that, from reading that chapter, you are able to take something of personal value for yourself that can help you in your own life's journey. I also hope that I get to meet you personally one day at one of my talks and that you can share with me some of your own experiences and the wisdom that you have learned through living your unique life.

Small Steps
Big Outcomes

- Appreciate what you have while you have it.

- Motivation, patience, and persistence.

- Most things in life, even the ones we don't want, have a positive side.

- I no longer take the good things in life for granted as they can be snatched away suddenly and unexpectedly, therefore, it's important to thoroughly appreciate what you have while you have it.

- I am grateful I have the opportunity to mobilise on two legs again.

- I have learned to appreciate the positive things in life and the wonderful people that I have come into contact with.

- It's great to be treated like a normal person and entitled to be myself.

- The way I see myself is more important than how others see me.

- I feel like myself again and this consciousness is uplifting.

- Being back on two legs again reveals both social differences and practical differences in day-to-day life.

- Enjoy just the simple things in life.

- Importance of friendships.

- The significance of time spent in solitude and with others.

Chapter 11
Motivation and Persistence

- What I visualised when setting my goals has become a reality and this transpired through a combination of resilience, adaptation, and motivation, as well as patience, determination and persistence.

- Goal oriented personality.

- Motivation, patience and persistence helps me to grow as a person.

- An ordinary woman forced to look within to find strengths to help me evolve.

- Find and release that inner strength within you.

- Get the most you possibly can out of life.

- I appreciate the tremendous supports I have had and continue to have, yet it is up to me how I choose to continue moving forward along the road ahead.

- Do you want to take control of the direction in which your life unfolds?

- Motivation is the energy source necessary for our functioning.

- Persistence is the determination to forge forward despite difficulties or opposition.

Chapter 12

Valuable Lessons

In many ways, this chapter is the most important and most valuable chapter in the book. When you go through extreme adversity, years of challenges and then eventually triumph you cannot do that without learning a lot a valuable life lessons and also experiencing a lot of personal growth in the process.

At various points throughout my story, I have mentioned some of the learnings that I thought were appropriate to mention at that point, but here in this chapter I will try to pull together the range of lessons I learned and hopefully do that in a way that will be of value to you in your own life.

The various principles and strategies that I discuss here are not some textbook theories, they are real lessons learnt through real experiences acquired over many years of both failure and success and eventually achievement of real goals by a real person, probably a lot like you, who just happened to be thrown into the deep end of life and had to learn how to survive and triumph.

Things can go wrong for anyone regardless of your health, wealth, education or background. None of us are immune to the challenges life entails and you do not have to have suffered from a major crisis to connect with my experiences. If you are lucky enough to survive a traumatic accident like mine, then that means that life is continuing for you from a point where it could have easily ended instead. To a large degree it is up to you just how life will continue. You can choose to draw negative energy or positive energy from your survival. I found from my own experience that survival leads me to recognising my true capabilities and to doing things that I had never imagined before. I believe that often it is the challenges you face and conquer in life that reveal the person you really are and that could be a person that no-one guessed was hiding inside you.

Are you a train wreck waiting to happen? Following trauma, I have discovered strengths within me that I have drawn upon to enable me to overcome monumental challenges, exceed expectations and live a fulfilling successful life. By reading what I have learnt, may it be an incentive for you to discover your strengths and capabilities without having to experience a traumatic event.

Chapter 12
Valuable Lessons

That leads me to the second lesson I learned, and that is best summed up in one of my favourite sayings: "We are all a bit like a teabag, we don't know how strong we are until we are dipped into hot water." I certainly had no idea how to cope with losing a leg, having my brain smashed in and parts of my brain removed, breaking my spine in five places and all the other things that resulted from my encounter with the solid train. The truth is that I had never even thought about it. I had been coasting along having a pretty good life with a good-looking future. I had a few minor ups and downs like anyone else but nothing like this. The lesson is that if you end up being put into a challenging situation, don't ever underestimate your own ability to triumph.

The next lesson I learned was the value of setting goals when you are trying to improve your life. Start with small goals and work your way up until you have a really inspiring goal. Achieving the small goals gives you confidence and encouragement to set a larger goal. I found by setting inspiring goals it gave me drive, purpose and motivation.

Once I started setting challenging goals, I soon had to learn another lesson, and that was to not be influenced by the negativity of others. There was never any shortage of people who were more than happy to tell me that I would never achieve my goals. They were happy to tell me that my goals were totally unrealistic. In fact, some of the experts told my family that my goals were so unrealistic that they were proof that the injuries to my brain had robbed me of my ability to judge reality. I wonder what they would think now if they found out that I have achieved every one of those goals. If I had listened to them my life would be so much less than it is now. I had to be prepared to believe in myself and what I knew I could do, regardless of whether other people supported me or opposed me. I firmly believe that we each have to take responsibility for our own outcomes and be prepared to do whatever we need to do in order to make our goals a reality.

Sometimes the people that are opposing you are people who believe that they are doing it for your own good. When this happens, I thank them for their concern but agree to disagree. I am never going to give up on my goals just because someone else cannot believe in them or in me, even if that opposition is motivated by what they perceive to be caring for my best interests.

When it comes to experts, I think they can be of great value. The right expert can open doors for you and guide you towards your goal. But equally, the wrong expert can lead you down the wrong path and waste your time or worse. I believe in finding experts that I believe in and who also believe in me. When I find such an expert, I will work with them to achieve my goal. That strategy has served me well and, in fact, that is the strategy I used to get back onto two legs again.

When it comes to goal setting there are a number of different theories out there. I don't follow theories. Instead, I follow what I have found to work in the real world. For example, there are some people today who preach that simply believing in your goals is enough to make them happen, but I do not believe in that. It has been my experience that goals become reality by a combination of belief, focus, hard work, strategy and persistence. Believing in your goal is a valuable ingredient to success but just believing is not enough on its own, you have to actually make it happen. Studies have revealed that willpower is greatly influenced by attitude. I believe that given the outcome

Chapter 12
Valuable Lessons

emotions have on willpower, being kind to ourselves will also help us to pursue and follow through with our goals.

Personally, I break my goal down into a series of small increments or steps and then I celebrate each step when I have achieved it. I find that this keeps me motivated and is especially important for long-term goals. I think that this makes a lot more sense than believing that it is just going to automatically happen for you simply because you set a goal. I have also found that setting small achievable goals keeps you focused and builds your confidence. I have found that by taking small steps it enabled me to be patient with the process and not waste valuable time, and to appreciate where I had come from. Small steps are my go-to words for moving forward. I believe that by taking action, small steps lead to big outcomes. Whatever difficulty you are facing there comes a time when you have to take the first step, determine your future and just go for it. I banished negativity by (figuratively speaking) taking a stance, making the first step, continuing to put one foot in front of the other and staying in motion.

I don't think it makes sense to just sit around and wait for success to happen. I think it makes more sense to learn how to recognise opportunity when it comes along and to develop the habit of seizing such opportunities and doing the work needed to make sure you truly capitalise on the opportunity. Sometimes opportunity comes along in disguise, so you have to be on the ball and open-minded if you are to recognise it. I have certainly discovered that crisis, in whatever form or however large or small, creates opportunity and it is important for us to be aware of this and have the courage to run with it.

Small Steps
Big Outcomes

Even if you jump on a great opportunity, you are still highly likely, at times, to experience some setbacks, especially if your goals are big, inspiring goals. In my journey to getting back onto two legs again I had sixteen years of setbacks. One of the most common questions I get from people is how I coped with so much failure and disappointment and still be able to get up and keep trying. Well, I think that having experienced that amount of disappointment, and learning how to cope with it, truly qualifies me as being proficient in how to handle setbacks and so I'd like to share with you some of the techniques that worked for me.

My first strategy is to not take setbacks personally. I have heard people make comments along the line that the universe is giving them a hard time. Or even making comments such as: *those sorts of things always happen to me*. I believe that the universe is not targeting you, me, or anyone else for problems. There is no rule out there that says you should be singled out as someone who always gets more than your fair share of difficulties. Problems, setbacks, and difficulties are simply a normal part of life and happen to most of us from time to time. You don't need to take them personally. The bigger your goals the more likely you are to experience some setbacks. It is just a by-product of setting yourself a more difficult task. Finding ways to overcome setbacks is what makes it so satisfying when you actually get what you are aiming for. If it were all too easy then it wouldn't mean anything to us. If it were easy, it would be a bit like breathing, often we would never notice or appreciate it, until for some reason it becomes hard to do.

My next strategy is to look at the way I am going about chasing my goal and then to ask myself if there is a better way I could be approaching the task. I know that it is unlikely that I will always be able to come up with the best possible way to do something

Chapter 12
Valuable Lessons

on the very first try. For me at times either my first efforts won't work at all or that if they do work, they won't work as well as they could and I'm guessing that it is probably the same for you. With that experience of those first efforts plus an open mind and some creative thinking you may come up with a much better strategy than the one that you were using.

Sometimes things go your way and sometimes they do not. When things are not going your way, it is very important to keep your attitude strong and healthy. I do this by looking for positives in what I have been doing and then use those positives to reinforce the idea that probably some things are actually going my way and that I just need to add to those small successes in order to build them into big successes. It's like running a hundred metre race – sometimes you win, sometimes you don't, but even failure is preparation for your next race.

I have found that one of the potential traps of failure is that it is easy to keep going over it in your mind and then, if you do that often enough, you will soon be depressed, and your self-confidence will be at a low. I get around this by taking some time out to do something that I really enjoy doing, something that takes my mind off the setback and puts me back into a positive mood.

Over my sixteen years of setbacks, I did have some very tough times where it was difficult to think positively and even the techniques I just mentioned were not working as well as they usually do. When such times would come, and I was at risk of slipping down to a negative or sinking attitude, I would often think of how far I had progressed and the multitude of obstacles I had conquered. I felt it was important to recognise small wins, acknowledge what I had achieved and be thankful that I was still alive and able to gradually move forward. I found that this strategy helped me to cope with things. It is a simple approach, but it worked for me! I think that it is important to find something that works for you and then, whatever it is, use it when you need it.

Sometimes a setback is due to something that is beyond your control. It does not make sense to me to worry about things that are beyond your control. If they are truly beyond your control, then worrying won't change anything for the positive so why waste your time worrying. I find it better to look for the things that I can control and that I believe will help me to move forward and make progress and then I put my energy into those things.

I have gone through a bunch of strategies for handling failure and setbacks, and I am sure that there are many other useful strategies too. Whichever strategies you use to handle failures and setbacks the important thing is that you find something that will help you to protect your good attitude. It was necessary for me to be adaptable whilst building and maintaining resilience. I approached my challenges with a positive attitude and continued to tell myself that I would be successful and believed this would greatly impact on the outcome. I simply had to do everything I possibly could and persist in doing whatever it took. These are the positive attitudes that helped me in moving forward toward my goals and eventually ensured I did achieve those goals. I am convinced that if you can maintain the right positive attitude then, sooner or later, you will find the strategies you need to find and take the action you need to take, to succeed at almost anything.

Another difficulty that I have had to deal with over the years is intense pain. I have experienced pain due to the various injuries

Chapter 12
Valuable Lessons

from the accident itself. I have experienced a lot of pain from the numerous operations that I have had over the years. I have experienced extreme pain during the months in which I was lengthening my femur bone to make it long enough for osseointegration. And then there is the very strong reoccurring pain known as phantom limb pain that I still experience at seemingly random times.

Normally the nerves in the various areas of your body are connected to areas in the brain where pain and other sensations are registered. When a limb is traumatically removed those connections in the brain can be scrambled in a way that confuses your brain. In my case, that means that the receptors in my brain, that formerly connected with my left leg, now do not have their normal job to do. This leads to neurons in that receptor area firing at certain times resulting in feelings of intense pain in a limb that is no longer connected to the body. I have tried all the known techniques for treating this type of pain, otherwise known as phantom pain, but they have not helped. I have bouts of extreme pain in a limb that no longer exists and therefore I have no way to ease that pain. I have accepted that this is likely to be something that I will always have for the rest of my life. Fortunately, it does not come every day, but when it does it is totally debilitating.

No sane person wants pain and those who are regular pain sufferers have their own ways of coping. In my case I prefer to be on my own when I am in pain. I have researched the way others have successfully removed or reduced their pain and some of those methods have worked for some of my pain. One example I have trialled is mirror therapy which involves the use of a mirror to develop reflective illusion and assist with visual imagery of an amputated limb in order to trick the brain into believing the limb is still attached. Apparently, the visual component leads to less phantom limb pain, but unfortunately with me it has not worked so far. I am afraid I cannot offer you any magic formula for getting rid of all pain. I have tried to distract my thoughts away from the pain and engage myself in some form of activity, but this also has not worked. If you know of a method that really works then please write to me and let me know. I would be very happy to find a solution to this problem.

Sometimes I am amazed at just how much physical and emotional pain I have had to deal with during my life and I admit that at times I ask: "Why me?" I think that it just isn't fair. Sometimes I have gotten to the point where I thought that I just could not cope with it anymore. But then I think about how my quality of life would be so much worse if I did not have all the operations and bone lengthening and so on. At the end of the day, I have succeeded in getting back on two legs and because of that I have gotten a normal life back and feel like Marny again. Therefore, I know that it has been worth it. Just the same, I truly hope that I do not have to experience much more. Hopefully, most of the pain is behind me.

I believe that you must have the determination to chase your dreams and goals, the process is all about learning and having the courage to think without limitations. I had the determination to pursue the direction that I felt would guide me to achieving my goals, knowing there would be difficulties. I felt that it was crucial to be patient and simply take one step at a time as often there were a few things involved to achieve. On achieving my goals, the doors of opportunity were swung open. After many years of sacrifices, focus, efforts, and resilience, I started to be rewarded. I am aware that success often takes time, so patience is required. The courage and determination required to change

Chapter 12
Valuable Lessons

your life can be found much easier when you remain focused while also being kind to yourself. We are all amazing individuals with a potential that is defined mainly by our way of thinking.

I think that it is so important to regularly stop and think just what I do have in my life. I have had my share of hardship, but things could easily have been much worse for me. I was unfortunate to have my accident, but I was fortunate to survive and recover so well. I am glad that I persisted when others told me to give up and I often look from where I am today and think of the life that I have had and then compare that to others who have been in a serious accident and unfortunately ended up so much worse off than I have. Regardless of our own difficulties, I think that if we have a good look around, we can usually find someone who is far worse off. I have found it really helps me when I become aware of that, and it brings home to me how fortunate I have been to be able to move forward and continue to do the things that I have done over the years.

I now get great pleasure in being able to do some of the simple things I took for granted before my accident. I am amazed at being so lucky to be able to do those things again and to know that I will be able to continue doing them for the years to come.

I am so relieved and happy when I often stop to think how lucky I am to be able to control the left side of my body. Initially after my accident my left side was paralysed, but over a short period of time full function returned. My left side is weaker than it was and will always remain weaker, but the functionality is there and remains. Because of that return of functionality, I can still play my violin, drive a car, sit and walk unsupported. I am so grateful for that.

Small Steps
Big Outcomes

The medical experts initially predicted that, due to my brain injuries, I would need twenty-four-hour care for the rest of my life, yet my brain totally recovered, and I have been living independently since the year after the accident, which I am so grateful for.

I have already described in detail what it means to me to be able to walk on two legs again and I am so grateful that I can.

I returned to my nursing profession nearly three years after my accident and have been working as a registered nurse ever since and I am so grateful for that. I also realise that in the long term I may need to find areas that are less intense physically on my body and I am actively working towards that goal.

I have been playing the violin virtually all my life and have loved every minute of it. I continue to play the violin in a variety of musical genres, and I am always looking to stretch my musical experience and ability. Music has been a huge part of my life and I am so grateful for that.

I have had great pleasure from staying in contact with life-long friends and in meeting new friends who have a positive impact in my life, and I am so grateful for that.

Sure, I have had my share of challenges, but I have so much to be grateful for and I realise that I am so much luckier than the many people who, for whatever reasons, did not recover from major injuries and trauma. I am now looking forward to using my experiences to help others get the most out of their life so that they do not have to have a catastrophe in order to fully wake them to their potential.

Chapter 12
Valuable Lessons

Our strength of character remains dormant until it is ignited. We do not know all of the potential possible directions our lives could, and possibly should have taken ... but I feel it is important to fight for things that give meaning to my life.

Small Steps
Big Outcomes

LESSONS

1. I believe in the strength of the human spirit.

2. Most of us have the choice to either accept or reject limitations. Often your choices and actions can determine your quality of life that you will live.

3. Frustration, correctly channelled, can be a very powerful motivator.

4. Keep moving forward, one step at a time.

5. The importance of gratitude.

6. Have a positive and productive mental attitude to help steer the direction of your life.

7. The importance of setting goals, developing strategies and staying on course, regardless of setbacks and obstacles.

8. Do not take for granted the simple or good things in life.

9. Fully appreciate what you have.

10. Solitude can be a good friend at times.

11. Life is not always fair, but it is up to me to work with what life throws me and to then make the best of it.

12. If you end up being put into a very challenging situation, don't ever underestimate your own ability to triumph.

13. I have learned to trust my instincts and live a life true to myself, not the life others presume I should have. Courage is required to be true to yourself and at times it takes an enormous amount of courage. I have found that by

Chapter 12
Valuable Lessons

withdrawing from the expectations of others it then allows you to go with your heart. Having the courage to then follow your heart is where genuine happiness lies.

14. The value of setting goals when you are trying to improve your life.

15. I wasn't deterred by the negativity of others …
    - I believed in myself.
    - I took responsibility for my own outcomes.
    - I was prepared to do whatever I needed to do in order to make my goals a reality.

16. I believe that when something bad happens you have three choices: let it define you; let it destroy you; or let it strengthen you.

17. Small steps can create BIG outcomes.

GOAL SETTING

1. Goals become reality by a combination of belief, focus, hard work, strategy and persistence, but you have to actually make it happen.

2. Willpower and attitude.

3. Be kind to yourself.

4. Break the goal down into a series of small steps.

5. Celebrate small wins to keep motivated, focused and to build confidence.

6. Recognise opportunities ... seize opportunities ... capitalise on opportunities.

7. Be attentive and open minded.

Chapter 12
Valuable Lessons

STRATEGIES

1. I don't take setbacks personally ... they are simply a normal part of life and can happen from time to time.

    - Finding ways to overcome setbacks is what makes it so satisfying when you actually get what you're aiming for.

2. Look at the way I am going about chasing my goal and then ask myself if there is a better way I could be approaching the task.

    - Have an open mind.
    - Creative thinking.

3. When things are not going my way, it is very important to keep my attitude strong and healthy.

    - Look for the positives.
    - Celebrate small wins.

4. Take some time out – do something you really enjoy.

5. What is the silver lining? How can the positive aspects be utilised?

6. Identify small wins and acknowledge your achievements.

7. Look for the things that I can control and that I believe will help me move forward.

8. Maintain courage and self-belief, persist in chasing my dreams and be determined to achieve my goals while keeping a positive attitude in order to keep me moving towards my goal.

9. Find something that will help to protect my good positive attitude:

    - Celebrating small wins, playing music, phoning and meeting up with a friend.
    - I continued to live my life and to be involved with my interests.

10. I had to have the determination to chase my dreams and goals. The process is all about learning and having the courage to think without limitation. I believe you need to:

    - Be resilient, adaptive, and determined.
    - Be kind to yourself.
    - Acknowledge that your way of thinking can at times define your true potential.
    - Take one step at a time.
    - Realise that some things do not happen straight away. Success often takes time, so patience is required.
    - Have courage and be determined to succeed.
    - Remain focused on what you want to achieve.

Chapter 12
Valuable Lessons

I AM GRATEFUL FOR

1. Surviving.

2. Being able to still do some of the simple things I took for granted.

3. How lucky I am to be able to control the left side of my body.

4. Living independently.

5. Being able to walk on two legs again.

6. Returning to work in my nursing profession.

7. Having my left hand still and able to continue playing my violin.

8. Staying in contact with life-long friends and in meeting new friends.

Life is too short to simply sit back and watch it go by.

There is a hidden strength within us, and life can be exceptional when we tap into that and discover our true potential.

Don't be afraid to fail because through failure you learn to succeed. Rethinking your approach to something is a powerful tool for success.

All of your life experiences, be they good or bad, are important factors that makes you unlike any other individual. Take control of the direction in which your life unfolds. Value all the positive aspects in your life, including your own capabilities and amazing self.

Chapter 13

My Beneficial Traits

If I wanted to be all that I could be and achieve the great outcomes I was capable of then there were a few things that I believed would increase my chances of success.

Many people have achieved amazing things and they are likely to have a few things in common. Obviously, I am talking from a woman's perspective, and I am relating to what has worked for me. Following are examples that I have recognised and developed within myself. You may also like to discover your strengths and elaborate on them to highlight your capabilities or possibilities.

1. RESILIENCE

None of us really know how we will react until we face hardship. I had to face my situations directly so I could address what I was dealing with. My view of resilience is the ability to deal with changes and challenges that unexpectedly occur in life and how thoughts and actions will influence the outcome. The process of adapting well, being flexible and moving forward throughout difficult experiences. Stressful events or adverse situations cannot always be prevented, but my capacity to deal with these challenges has been strengthened. I have an optimistic outlook on life and accept that life is about losses as much as it is wins. I view my challenges with positive actions, instead of inaction, avoidance or escaping. Resilience has enabled me to deal more effectively with the multiple challenging situations I have been confronted with and has been enhanced in several ways, mainly through acknowledging and focusing on my strengths, having a positive mindset and being confident in my capabilities. I aim my attention on possibilities and explore how I can transform my strengths into something superb.

Research has shown that resilience is ordinary, not extraordinary. People commonly demonstrate resilience. Being resilient does not mean that you don't experience difficulty or distress. Emotional pain and sadness can be present in people from all walks of life and not only those who have suffered major adversity or trauma in their lives. The road to resilience is likely to involve considerable emotional distress. I dealt with my emotional pain and sadness by working towards things that would give me pleasure and improve the quality of my life. Regardless of how long it took, I enjoyed the fact that I was progressing (even though it was only minimal at times) and I continued to remain active outside with sports.

My understanding of resilience is that it is not a trait that people either have or do not have. It involves beliefs, behaviours, thoughts and actions that can be learned and developed. I have developed and maintained my current beliefs, behaviours, thoughts and actions since I was an infant. My background has made me stronger, and I know I can positively deal with things thrown in my path. Fundamentally, resilience is about assembling what is within us to make it through and possibly transform what is to become.

There are a number of skills required to build resilience and some that have worked for me include attempting to remain confident, calm and consciously aware of living in the moment, embracing

Chapter 13
My Beneficial Traits

change and controlling how I react and respond to given situations, nourishing and rewarding myself, maintaining and building positive social relationships and practicing my abilities. Ultimately, I focus on my strengths and positively manage deficient areas to stimulate a successful outcome.

Overall, it was necessary for me to roll with the punches, realise that the bad times will pass and be aware to not be too tough on myself. Good mindsets can be learned and learning to be more resilient can benefit everyone.

My resilience is built from: my optimism, by focusing on what is going well for me and what I am grateful for; my flexible thinking and viewing stressful events as a challenge and not a threat; ensuring I made changes, however small, to improve my health, through good quality sleep, diet and exercise; and making connections, building positive relationships and putting valuable time into those friendships. In moments of stress, I gravitated towards what I believed would relax me at that point in time. Activities ranged from simply being on my own, listening to music, getting outside into nature or whatever I felt was necessary at that moment.

I feel a need to capitalise on the traits I have developed. Resilience has enabled me to cope better with major stress and minor hassles, successfully overcome many challenges and has allowed me to perceive challenges and setbacks as manageable. I will not be defeated by life!

I feel that adopting a resilient approach to achieve goals and overcome challenges enabled me to deal more effectively with each situation. I believe that all of us are capable of being resilient, in varying degrees, especially when push comes to shove.

2. ADAPTABILITY

My experiences have helped me to understand that crisis does create opportunities and that I am capable of adapting. I unexpectedly experienced trauma that resulted in changes to almost every aspect of my life. By being adaptable, I was still capable of and willing to change my approach to doing things to suit the various situations and different conditions I was faced with. We adjust in various ways to alterations in our life, and opportunities are created when we adapt to change and take action.

People adapt, both to the best and worst that can occur. Change ignites emotions and keeps us dynamic and fresh. It was necessary for me to adapt to change, forgo my previous capabilities and focus on my habits that previously helped me to define my success and prevent me from deteriorating due to lack of action. I have to be resourceful and not get stuck on one solution to my problems. I am open to opportunities and strive to improve through minor adjustments and not be stranded with the one-size-fits-all solution. I also feel it is important not to blame anyone for my setbacks and I do not hold any grudges towards those who undermine me. I remain proactive while attempting to absorb and understand what is occurring and move on.

It is just not possible for me to return to my normal biological state and my only evident option is to forge ahead with creativity. Being adaptable has certainly made my life easier. I continue to work towards my goal and do not flit from one thing to the next. I think my adaptability is firmly connected with my resilience and perseverance. I keep going, even when the going is tough. I needed to concentrate on what I wanted, discipline

Chapter 13
My Beneficial Traits

myself and to remain motivated to complete what I had set out to achieve. Be it my personal achievements, music development or work environment, I felt the need to improvise and not overthink or second-guess things. I grab opportunities when they arise as they may not come again. It can be natural at times to resist change, but with some of the changes I have experienced I have responded positively by changing my outlook and behaviour and started with small steps. Yes, I have been disappointed when my plans changed but I responded enthusiastically even when I did not feel like it. For example, when I lost my job, I bounced forward by taking positive actions on a daily basis until I was employed in an area which I enjoyed more and enhanced my nursing experiences.

I become creative at problem solving and research has suggested that you are better able to cope with problems if you are able to think of some solutions. When I encounter a new challenge, I think about some of the possible ways of solving this problem and make note of them. I target my energy on the results I want, not on the difficulties I am facing. Through experimentation I then focus on developing logical ways to deal with and work through my problem. It is important for me to have a survivor attitude, not see myself as a victim in negative situations and consistently look for ways to resolve it. I cannot always be in control of my circumstances and events that happen, but I can be in control of how I respond and react. I believe that by having this attitude I will influence the situation favourably.

I have certainly benefited from being adaptable and being open to finding various solutions to my problems be it in my personal or working life. I have bounced forward from adversity more quickly, I am happier and more satisfied with my life, I am better at handling career transitions and am more valuable to my employer and those surrounding me.

I will continue to learn and be willing to discover new methods, procedures and ways of achieving things. Try something that is different. Take on a new task. Speculate new information and draw conclusions. It is easy to tell ourselves that we do not have time. Our life is not a dress rehearsal. I encourage you to respond with energy and enthusiasm to new challenges, the unexpected and the unfamiliar.

Because of my accident, I am driven to transform my life in ways that are profoundly positive. What have I got to lose? It has been a tough road, but some great opportunities have been ignited as a result of dealing with adversity and challenging situations. Sometimes a failure is needed to open our eyes to opportunities that were present and in front of us the whole time. I have found that crisis does create opportunities.

Dealing with challenges requires strength of character and may require you to burrow into resources deep within you that you never knew were present, but I can assure you that they do exist. May you also be able to adapt and find alternative ways to proceed and forge forward from problems or situations requiring great effort.

3. DETERMINATION

I regard determination to be a positive emotion that helps me to be more motivated to achieve my goals. I see determination as unyielding intent to achieve a desired outcome and represents what I am willing to do to accomplish the result I want. I had to persevere in working towards challenging goals despite

Chapter 13
My Beneficial Traits

obstacles. I had the willpower to be successful, set ambitious goals and persist in working towards accomplishing them.

My determination stemmed from being intensely committed, regularly reviewing and realigning my actions, and working from my strengths. It wasn't always easy, but I had to give nothing less than 100% as I didn't rely on luck. I was also aware of avoiding distractions and realised that at times the road to success has many obstacles that makes you struggle to make just a small impact. I have found that it is necessary for me to create routine and structure and efficiently manage limited resources.

My determination required focus and it was important for me to manage my focus so I could actively guide my thoughts towards positive outcomes and solutions, and away from negativity and fear. I focused on finding a positive in every situation. At times this was difficult and at such times I reminded myself about what was going well for me. Ultimately, the quality of my life depended on what I chose to focus on. What will you focus on? The problem or the solution, the positive or the negative, the past or the future.

My determination remained focused on what I wanted to achieve, and this kept me moving forward. I also needed to keep my emotions under control throughout my journeys. My emotions ranged from eagerness to get things done and to being angry with the frustrations I encountered – which could demotivate me. When I was confronted with obstacles, I did not let this deter me from what I wanted to achieve and redirected my actions and thoughts along another path. When difficulties arose, despite what was put in front of me, my determination helped me to keep forging forward. If something didn't work, I continued to be driven to be successful and viewed the setback as a diversion, not an end. I viewed my will to keep going as an essential component of what I have achieved, despite the odds against me. Focus helps me to set the direction and achieve the target I am aiming for.

4. POSITIVE ATTITUDE

I relate to having a positive attitude as being optimistic and expecting good outcomes. Having a positive attitude is greatly beneficial for me but negative thoughts surface sometimes. I am positive more than I am negative and am convinced that my outlook contributed to much of my success and how I approached it.

I believe language can also shape your thoughts and at times my use of language also reflects a positive approach. I would refer to my problem as a challenge. I view challenge as a positive word because it is something I have to rise to and sooner or later would make me stronger and improve my situation. When I notice negative thoughts, I stop them in their tracks and identify the positives in my given situation and am grateful for them. Do you rise to the challenge?

It was important that I did not worry about the things that I was unable to control, didn't make excuses and took ownership of things that I was able to manage and control. Other ways that help me to maintain a positive attitude is to think positive thoughts, structure my day, surround myself with positive people, determine how I respond to the outside world and choosing if my experience is positive or negative and react accordingly. For example, I lost my job and was officially informed of this via email. Despite the emotions I was feeling, I chose how I reacted to this and saw it as an opportunity for

Chapter 13
My Beneficial Traits

bigger and brighter things. I had to be optimistic, see what could be done and sculpted my actions to mirror my imagination.

To maintain a positive attitude, I believe it is important for me to take time out. As I am not in a financial position to travel regularly or travel as often as I would like to, I have a home holiday where I do things that I enjoy, relax, and somehow break the monotony of daily living and routines.

I hope that you can explore ways for cultivating a positive mindset and can identify the multiple benefits that can be obtained from approaching life with a positive outlook.

5. PATIENCE

I understand that patience is the ability to remain calm while you are waiting for a specific outcome that you either want or need.

I, like most others, can lose my patience occasionally. Whether it be with overcoming serious setbacks in my life, circumstances that are beyond my control or another person's demands and failings. At such times I attempt to reframe the situation with my thoughts, be thankful for how far I have come and not be desperate for better circumstances immediately.

My experiences have disclosed that patience helped me to achieve my goals. Attaining my independence, work pursuits and mobility status was a long journey, and I grew in strength, learned from and gained valuable insight from each of these separate areas. Intense diligence was required, and it was imperative that I activated the starting point and got things done to cross the finish line.

Small Steps
Big Outcomes

In my working and personal life, I have identified that by being patient I am viewed more positively by managers, co-workers, family and friends. The outcome of this is I remain focused, productive and work well within a team environment. At times, others have interpreted my being patient to signify that I am a pushover, which is an incorrect assumption. I am confident to politely show my displeasure when someone is unnecessarily undermining me, or I respectfully agree to disagree. When appropriate, I establish strong boundaries while remaining polite and assertive.

Sometimes I have to be patient with daily hassles, hardships of life or interpersonal relationships. I view daily hassles as circumstances that are outside of my control. These states of affairs do not contribute to my personal goals, but I am able to maintain self-discipline despite these and give my attention to details required. I have the patience to overcome serious setbacks in my life and the ability to work towards a long-term goal whether it be personal, such as regaining my independence and walking again, or professional, such as returning to work and contributing positively to specialised areas. I refer to interpersonal patience as being patient with others, their demands and their flaws. In these situations, I am aware of how my words and actions will affect the situation, actively listen and be empathetic. Just waiting it out and hoping for the best is not an option for me.

Fortunately, I have been able to endure some difficult circumstances. Patience not only allowed my life to be more pleasant in the here and now, but it also helped in paving the way for my future to be more satisfying and successful. Patience helped me to achieve my goals. Sometimes my road to

Chapter 13
My Beneficial Traits

achievement was a long one and with patience I had to be willing to walk it one small step at a time.

6. PERSISTENCE

I have heard that persistence pays off. Persistence often refers to when you continue to do and work at something regardless of it being difficult or when others are against it, despite the setbacks, fatigue or frustration you may experience.

One example of me being persistent is achieving my goal of walking again even though it took me sixteen years to conquer. When I experienced a setback, I found another way to approach things. I was then able to adjust and adapt my action plan and felt this would increase my chances of success. My tenacity paid off and has made living a lot easier for me.

When I have my mind set on something and I'm determined to achieve it, to help with the continual flow of my efforts, I begin with something simple and relatively easy. I am then able to persevere and gradually achieve what I set out to accomplish. With each attempt I make, I think I am one step closer to success. When I notice small differences between where I am and where I was, my motivation is escalated, and I keep trying again and again. Comprehensively, I visualise the outcome I want, and I'm driven to move forward along the route that will lead to transformation and a better world for me.

I had to accept that achieving my main goals was not going to happen overnight and achieving them would result from strong, consistent actions in the direction of new horizons. Transitioning from critical situations is a journey and that journey is not always easy or straightforward.

Persistence has taught me the value of success and that it is not always easy to achieve. It has enlightened me about the ongoing dedication that is needed to make something happen and the amount of hard work necessary. To be successful I had to be prepared to do everything I possibly could. I discovered that experiencing failure along the long road to success did not mean I had failed. Failure would only occur if I let my negative experiences cause me to quit.

7. BELIEF

Believing I can be triumphant in my goals is beneficial but the mere thought of believing on its own is not enough, I *have to make it happen* and do everything I possibly can to create the result I am aiming for. I would not have set off on a journey to achieve my aspirations if I did not believe that I had the ability to get there. I am of the opinion that if I go into something with the positive attitude of *I can do it* rather than *this can't be done*, I am more likely to achieve the results I want.

In believing that I would successfully achieve my goals, I grasped at every opportunity and was stimulated to take action and sustain my efforts over extended periods of time. My belief was reinforced when I continued to achieve my goals and saw setbacks as part of the process and just kept going. Although I wanted what I was aiming for sooner than when they could reasonably be obtained, my needs provided me with goals and established priorities.

I know what I am capable of, and I continue to believe in my internal strength and capabilities. Despite all the setbacks, this belief is a positive feeling that empowered me and gave me confidence to face the challenges I was confronted with. I have

Chapter 13
My Beneficial Traits

come to know that by believing that things will work out for the best, it will create an attitude that is optimistic and healthy, that can assist to facilitate the desired result.

Research has revealed that self-belief is thought of as a very influential motivator and regulator of our behaviour. Believing in what I was capable of was significant as ultimately it determined my quality of life. The belief in my capabilities has resulted in me developing strong confidence in my judgement and abilities.

I have found that belief can fuel expectations and intentions. Research has shown that our habitual thoughts have a compelling force on our experiences. I was constantly focused on moving forward one small step at a time. My thoughts and beliefs strongly contributed to me overcoming obstacles and dealing with emotional, physical and psychological demands. I hope you are able to recognise that your thoughts and what you focus on will have a profound effect on outcomes.

We all have something that we are uniquely good at and has the potential to make us more positive, happier, and creative. When challenges arise, they disguise an extensive source of opportunity if they are looked at from the right perspective. I encourage you to discover your strengths and focus on utilising these whenever necessary.

8. COURAGE

What would you do if you had no fear? Taking risks does not mean you will be doing careless things, but it does mean making planned decisions.

My courage to forge forward was strengthened by my WHY, which has helped to pull me through some difficult times. I am results orientated and I have the courage to continue to pursue what I am aiming for despite setbacks. Trauma and crisis forced me to think of my why and subsequently revealed unprecedented opportunities to transform my life and continue moving forward.

I understand that the meaning of courage can be different for everyone. There are various kinds of courage that range from physical strength and staying power, to mental strength and the introduction of something new or different. I will relate to my courage in persevering in the face of adversity. I had to keep strong within myself and made the decision to keep moving forward. Courage did not always roar and be dominant for me. Sometimes it was listening to that little voice within me that said *try again* and devise ways in which I could find an approach that was over, under, around or through a barrier to enable me to breakthrough. Courage helped me to accomplish great things that continue to impact positively on my life.

I have found that courage allowed me to confront troublesome situations and difficulties appropriately. I had to think things through beforehand in order to find the right balance as I was aware that I couldn't achieve what I wanted straight away.

I had courage because I believed I could do it and consistently took action in the face of adversity. My courage increased my confidence, allowed me to see things differently and believe in my abilities and brought happiness into my life. It can be challenging when you step outside the security of familiarity, however, I realised that having the courage to challenge myself this way has enabled me to discover resources within me that I never knew I had.

Chapter 13
My Beneficial Traits

9. GRATITUDE

I see gratitude as taking time to acknowledge and appreciate all the positive things in my life. Instead of ruminating on the negative aspects I identify what is going well for me. I have discovered that when you promote an outlook of gratitude you open your mind to more positivity that consequently fuels success.

Gratitude empowered my determination and helped to increase my level of happiness throughout ongoing hardships. Over the years, amongst a variety of other advantageous outcomes, my feeling of appreciation has also assisted me to deal with adversity, strengthen my positive emotions and made me more optimistic.

Gratitude does not cost me anything, doesn't take much of my time and the benefits are enormous. Gratitude has impacted on many aspects of my life in relation to my health, emotions, career and social dynamics. Gratitude has improved my physical and emotional well-being and opened the door to professional relationships and improved my self-esteem. Effectively, gratitude created social networks, helped me to work towards my goals and challenges and, in the long term, provided me with stronger skills for dealing with life's hardships.

I have come to understand the valuable effects of gratitude and believe it to be more than a feeling of being thankful. It is recognition and a deep appreciation for something or someone that generates positivity that is longer lasting.

I am grateful that my focus has shaped my life and helped me to forge forward. The quality of my life would have been left to chance if I did not consciously direct my focus on big outcomes.

Small Steps
Big Outcomes

Chapter 13
My Beneficial Traits

1. **Resilience** – Resilience is about our beliefs, our behaviours, our thoughts and our actions in the face of adversity. Are you able to utilise your skills and strengths to manage and recover from problems and challenges?

2. **Adaptability** – Crisis creates opportunities. Adjusting to different scenarios encompasses many different aspects and approaches. I certainly discovered that one size does not always fit and how important it is to seize opportunities that are created when we adapt to change and take action. I was flexible whist taking small steps in moving forward and my versatility enabled me to focus on solutions rather than problems.

3. **Determination** – This positive emotion directed me towards the outcome I wanted and required focus, revision and adjustment

4. **Positive Attitude** – I maintained a positive way of thinking and was optimistic. This mentality helped me to recognise opportunities and focus on the good side of things and the brighter side of life.

5. **Patience** – Allowed me to change my perspective and supported my endurance. It was a long and difficult road to successfully achieve what I was aiming for, and patience has not only helped me to conquer steep inclinations, but it has also enhanced my life.

6. **Persistence** – Finally, after sixteen years, persistence did pay off and my life was improved dramatically. Do not be afraid to fail because through failure you learn to succeed. Rethinking your approach to something is a powerful tool for success.

7. **Belief** – My positive beliefs certainly motivated me but simply believing was not going to help me, I had to do everything I possibly could to *make it happen.* Your thoughts and what you focus on will have a profound effect on outcomes.

8. **Courage** – It was necessary for me to be brave and confront obstacles head on, so I didn't waste some of my precious time and get to where I wanted to be. My cup is certainly half full. Despite ongoing obstacles, I was determined to keep moving forward, however long it took, and concentrate on where my actions will lead me. My courage to keep progressing was strengthened by my why, that revealed exceptional opportunities to change my life and continue moving forward. What is your why?

9. **Gratitude** – Life isn't always easy, but I can still identify and be grateful for the positive elements within my life. This has reinforced my belief that even bad experiences that you would have preferred to not have, can still have their upside if you keep your eyes open for that upside.

Chapter 14

A Few Last Thoughts

Thank you for taking the time to read my memoir. I appreciate that we live in a very busy world and time is our most valuable asset, so I am grateful that you have given up some of your time to discover parts of my story.

My experiences are adventures written to inspire you to overcome obstacles, so you have an opportunity to get what you want out of life.

My story is about an event that could have happened to anyone. On that particular Sunday night in the London Underground I was unfortunately in the wrong place at the wrong time. It is extremely rare for someone to survive such a horrific accident and I have now taken you on my journey from life support to recapturing life and living a fulfilling existence. I am hopeful that you have come to understand how small steps can create big outcomes. You can do it. Make it happen. It is about moving forward one small step at a time and celebrating small wins.

On a very personal note, I would like to say that going through the process of writing this memoir has been a wonderful experience for me. Taking the time to go over my life in a structured way has helped reinforce just how well life has treated me in so many ways. Writing this memoir has definitely been a valuable learning and healing experience for me.

Small Steps
Big Outcomes

I sincerely hope that spending the time to read my memoir has been a valuable use of time for you also. I have tried my best to share my story in a way that will positively influence you. I would love to hear how small steps in the right direction have created big outcomes for you and how you have used the challenges that you have come up against to carve a new life.

www.marnycringle.com.au

Conclusion

All of us have knowledge and experiences that others are not aware of but could benefit from. My story highlights how my outlook towards my given situation impacted on my life and what it did for me. I want to empower you to recognise and use your full potential and be determined to do what it takes to get the results you want so you can live a fulfilling life.

My journey through life has been very colourful and has entailed significant highs and awful lows. My accident also tested me and pushed me to my limits. My experiences mentioned, along with many others, is what defines me and makes me the woman I am today.

What you gain by achieving your goals is not as important as how you are transformed by achieving them. Life changing goals usually take a lot of time and effort, but because they change you for the better, you get the benefits for long after you have achieved them.

My experiences have defined me and made me who I am today. My unexpected accident has changed my life that has been transformed by my determination to keep moving forward and create a life that is an improvement on and more valuable than I had previously enjoyed. Life is not always fair and negative things can happen. Fortunately, I have been able to turn the difficulties I have been confronted with into opportunities and forge ahead into a future that is bright and rewarding.

Small Steps
Big Outcomes

My tremendous outcomes have resulted from me taking small steps to get to where I wanted to be. Through my results-orientated personal achievements, I worked with my strengths, positivity, resilience, adaptability and determination when conquering setbacks. I want to inspire you to get the most out of life and find the internal strength you need to overcome a challenge or reach your goal. Ultimately, this will allow you to positively move forward and enable you to make the most of any given situation you are faced with.

Many of us, at some stage of our lives, are faced with something that requires us to make a special effort. It is just a matter of how you deal with these demands and to be determined to overcome them either by success, acceptance, or both. With the right attitude you can overcome and be triumphant. Despite setbacks, it can be possible to progressively move forward one step at a time.

Many people react to stories of adversity because they awaken memories of something of what we are capable of and they inspire us, however briefly, to think of the possibilities in our own lives. I was not able to control all the elements of how my life unfolded but, like you, with the right attitude we can influence and have greater control over outcomes.

I encourage you to think thoughts of success, go confidently in the direction of your dreams and know that you have what it takes. Believe in yourself, you are capable of more than you realise.

All of our life experiences be they good or bad, are important factors that make us unlike any other individual. Take control of the direction in which your life unfolds. Value all the positive aspects in your life, including your capabilities and amazing self.

Conclusion
A Few Last Thoughts

I have recognised that my potential is uncapped. The best thing I have manifested from my experiences is a more powerful me. Struggles develop strength. Many of us will encounter barriers throughout our lives. Do not underestimate the power within you. Allow yourself to be all that you can be. You are capable of amazing things.

May you continue to forge forward, may your thoughts be limitless, and may you succeed in getting what you want out of life. It is okay to be unhappy with where you are as it can assist you to aim higher. You are capable and it is important to realise your strengths and use them wisely to achieve the best possible outcome.

Taking small steps is a powerful strategy for achieving success and making positive changes in your life.

Small steps, big outcomes emphasizes the idea that making consistent, incremental progress can lead to significant results over time. This approach can be applied to many different areas of life, such as personal development, health and fitness, or achieving a specific goal. By taking small, manageable actions each day, you can build momentum and create a positive feedback loop that helps you make progress towards your goals.

For example, if your goal is to improve your physical fitness, you might start by taking short walks every day and gradually increasing the distance you cover. If your goal is to save money, you might start by reducing your spending on small luxuries and putting the savings into a dedicated account. Over time, these small steps can add up to significant improvements in your health, wealth, or other areas of your life.

Small Steps
Big Outcomes

It's important to remember that the process of taking small steps towards your goals can sometimes be slow and steady, and that's okay. The key is to focus on consistency and progress, rather than trying to achieve everything at once.

When setting out to accomplish something I encourage you to take one step at a time towards your goal and direct your attention to solutions, positive results and outcomes. If your progress is obstructed in the coming days, weeks or months, I encourage you to believe that you are resilient, know that adaptability can enhance your situation and be determined to get the results you want.

CHOOSE YOUR FUTURE
If you are looking for control over your life, it's closer than you think.

ACHIEVE YOUR GOALS
One step at a time.

CELEBRATE SMALL WINS
It's easy to overlook the small wins, but together they make the biggest difference.

Acknowledgements

My adversity has stimulated extreme emotional growth and ignited my motivation to achieve many of my successes. My achievement has also resulted from the support and cooperation of others. During critical situations or whilst attempting to navigate through to where I was aiming, I was fortunate to be able to connect with people and appreciate those connections who were particularly important during my turning points.

My dear friends Kim and Paul have both encouraged me to write and speak for many years. They stimulated my desire to write this memoir, to help launch me into becoming a successful inspirational speaker and have provided ongoing support with the progression and development of my input into my story and personal life experiences. Your heart-warming and joyful friendship is uplifting. You are both an important part of my life and I am grateful for your friendship and support throughout my exciting journeys.

My community of Maitland has supported and advocated for me throughout one of the most difficult times in my life in the hope that I overcame the many obstacles I faced. I believe we all need a sense of belonging that is a human emotional need which ultimately connects us to the relationships we establish. I have grown up and developed within the welcoming community of Maitland who have contributed to the shaping of my identity and pride as a woman who has faced adversity. Feeling that I belonged encouraged me to fight for my survival and well-being. I will be forever thankful to my community as they have accepted me and made me feel as though I belong. Because I had a sense of belonging, I was encouraged to see the value in life and manage intensely painful emotions.

Just some of the many groups within the Maitland community who have supported me include the various Probus Clubs, View Club, National Seniors, Rotary, Catholic Diocese, Toastmasters, Kiwanis Club of East Maitland, St Joseph's College Lochinvar, and Sisters of St Joseph. People within these groups, who I regards as friends, continue to be supportive of me and I am appreciative of their embrace.

I would like to thank every person and organisation mentioned in my story. You have impacted positively on me and assisted me to get to where I am today. You have supported me unconditionally and contributed to my successful outcomes and the quality of my life. I am sincerely grateful for your support.

There are many other individuals and organisations that have supported me throughout my journey. If you are not mentioned please do not think that I have forgotten you or that I do not appreciate what you have done for me. My life has been positively enhanced by many and I am grateful for the support of everyone who has been a pillar of strength throughout my life in both the good times and the bad.

Thank you to a man who I met through music and has now passed away, Pedro, who also encouraged me to act on my intentions to write my story and helped me with suggestions initially when outlining my story and speaking ambitions.

Thank you to my dear friends from school, Tracy and Marian, who supported and assisted me when I chose to include details of what happened to me throughout my childhood and how best

Acknowledgements
A Few Last Thoughts

to articulate this. I greatly appreciate your support and friendship.

Friendships evolve through history and understanding. Having experienced extensive traumatic and painful times, I certainly know how valuable my loyal friends have been in supporting me throughout. Even through the worst of times friends are able to make you laugh. It is not always possible for them to physically be there, but any form of communication can provide strength and comfort during tough times.

I regard my friends as my family. It is difficult to mention all of my friends, but I am particularly referring to those who I remain in close contact with. Kim, Janice and Marian who I communicate with regularly, my dear school family Michelle, Jane and Patricia who are intensely engrained in my heart, my supportive community family, my expressive music family, my energetic tennis family, my uplifting amputee family, my embracing work family, and my loving extended family. You have stood by me and given me support, encouragement and determination to continue moving forward with my head above all the storms and whirlwinds of life. You have an exceptional place in my life. Our bond has developed so much over the years that it is cemented within me and will remain part of me.

Thank you to a friend who I connected with immediately, my colourful and welcoming publisher, Deborah, a successful and educated woman who is passionate in helping women evolve and generate an exciting life for themselves and those around them. You have provided me with so much insight and in conjunction with my editor you have assisted me immensely in constructing my story. Your ideas and suggestions are focused on the direction of what I want to reveal in order to make the greatest impact. Thank you also for introducing me to Business and Professional Women (BPW) and providing me with an opportunity for both personal and professional development, and to meet and socialise with other women while providing a valuable network. The first time I travelled interstate to speak was with BPW Caboolture who are a very welcoming, supportive and informative group. Thank you for opening my eyes and encouraging me to expand my wings.

We all have hidden reserves of potential. I want my story to positively influence you to discover your capabilities. My experiences have revealed to me that challenges are not an end point and should be addressed with the right mindset and methods, so they can be the beginning of something new, create opportunities and lead to other avenues and positive outcomes. My challenges have impacted me greatly and I would like my experiences to be a catalyst for change in others and help you to also move forward and discover your potential.

I hope I am able to assist you to get the most out of your life and gain as much as you possibly can from it, by continuing to move forward one step at a time while focusing on solutions, so you can realise and develop your full potential and achieve the best possible outcome.

Nearing the completion of this memoir I was fortunately introduced to an organisation to help direct me into a successful journey with speaking. I want to be transformed and learn how to successfully master my communication skills and become an inspirational speaker who provides immense value for others. I

Acknowledgements
A Few Last Thoughts

was very pleased to connect with the Pay It Forward And Profit group who are a remarkable team of speakers, trainers and facilitators who are highly regarded globally. I met with them via Zoom regularly and they assisted me to explore ways to serve my way to success. I am now on another journey where I am empowered to create value for those I come into contact with, positively impact the lives of others and ensure that everyone benefits.

So, after you put this book down, please remember to take time to appreciate every moment in your life – the good and the bad. Sometimes there will be tears. Sometimes there will be laughter. And if you are lucky, there will be friends to share it all with, as I have known throughout my life.

I think it is important to be happy, and to make others happy too. Make yourself a friend to the world. Do this for your new friend, Marny.

I want to encourage you to get the most out of life and gain as much as you possibly can from it … by continuing to move forward one step at a time … so you can realise and develop your full potential and achieve the best possible outcome.

At Bootcamp, March 2020

Life is full of possibilities, and we have the choice to celebrate it. Look for opportunities and find ways to reveal your strengths.

Life is a great adventure. Live the journey.

Extraordinary lives are created by ordinary people taking small steps that create big outcomes.

FORGE FORWARD from Adversity

I have found through personal experience that small steps can create big outcomes and are the key to achieving what you are aiming for. With my R.A.D. Conquest Method, you can experience empowerment in your life to get virtually anything you want no matter where you start from.

www.ingramcontent.com/pod-product-compliance
Lightning Source LLC
Chambersburg PA
CBHW071112160426
43196CB00013B/2544